Getting into

Pharmacy and Pharmacology Courses

Getting into guides

Getting into

Pharmacy and Pharmacology Courses

Bridget Hutchings
2nd edition

trotman | **t**

Getting into Pharmacy and Pharmacology Courses

This 2nd edition published in 2018 by Trotman Education, an imprint of Crimson Publishing Limited, 21d Charles Street, Bath BA1 1HX

© Crimson Publishing Ltd 2018

Author: Bridget Hutchings

First edition by Bridget Hutchings, 2014

British Library Cataloguing in Publication Data
A catalogue record for this book is available from the British Library

ISBN: 978 1 911067 76 4

Printed and bound in the UK by 4edge Limited

Contents

About the author

Bridget Hutchings studied for a BA Joint Honours degree in English and History at Keele University. After working in industry for four years, she returned to Keele to take a Postgraduate Certificate in Education. Bridget taught in several schools in the maintained and independent sectors in Staffordshire before moving to Exeter, initially as Head of English and later as Assistant Head with responsibility for Sixth Form. She is currently Head of Learning Support and Personal Tutor at MPW Birmingham, a role that has developed further her experience of the university application process.

Bridget's great-grandfather opened the first branch of Boots in Scarborough, North Yorkshire and was a pharmacist, her family connection giving her a personal interest in pharmacy and pharmacology.

Acknowledgements

My thanks go to the members of staff at MPW Birmingham who have shared their expertise in university applications and helped with research. I am also grateful to my family and friends for keeping me going while writing this new title in the series.

Grateful thanks to the following universities, which have been very helpful in providing information: Aston, Bradford, Keele, Kingston, Leeds, Manchester and Nottingham.

Particular thanks also go to these students currently taking an MPharm degree: Daniela Gennuso, Alisha Hussain, Qam, Isobel Sharma and Matthew Stibbs, and also to Raveena Gill and Jennifer Powley, qualified pharmacists. Thanks also to graduates Jessica Thompson, Jasdeep and Ruth. They have all given generously of their time to assist with this second edition.

Introduction

As a student deciding on a course that will determine your future career, the process of investigating which course will suit you best, narrowing down the choice of universities by their specific course content and entrance criteria and then embarking on the application process will all feel incredibly daunting! Having reached for this book, it is likely that you already have some interest in pharmacy or pharmacology but need to find out much more about the differences between them. This book is intended to give you a guided tour through all the important stages of research and application, from reading course criteria and visiting universities to filling in the all-important UCAS form and attending interviews, and to enable you not only to make a successful application to university but to have a clear insight into the next stages in your career. While it is no substitute for your own further research and practical experience, it will help you to decide whether pharmacy or pharmacology is a realistic option for you.

Introducing pharmacy and pharmacology

To ensure you are reading this book with a clear understanding of the differences between pharmacy and pharmacology and whether they are right for you, it is essential to clarify the following.

* Only a master's degree in pharmacy (MPharm), usually of four years' duration, accredited by the General Pharmaceutical Council (GPhC), will qualify a graduate, following the pre-registration placement and examination, to practise as a pharmacist. Pharmacists in England, Wales and Scotland are required to register with the GPhC, and those in Northern Ireland with the Pharmaceutical Society of Northern Ireland.
* A degree in pharmacology will not qualify you to practise as a pharmacist but will enable you to go into career areas which require a detailed understanding of the science of drugs and the impact they have on the human body. These areas may include researching and developing new drugs, analysing their effects and potential side effects. As a graduate, you may be working in educational establishments, pharmaceutical organisations and laboratories.
* While this book will focus on pharmacology on its own or as one subject in a Joint Honours degree, the study of pharmacology can be found in many biomedical disciplines.

Many universities will offer degrees in pharmaceutical science, which focuses on the design and development of new drugs; this book is not intended as a guide to these degree courses but may lead you to consider and then research this area as a viable alternative to pharmacy and pharmacology.

This book is divided into the following chapters.

Chapter 1 is intended to give you a strong understanding of all aspects of pharmacy and pharmacology so that you can be certain that one of them is right for you. It will define pharmacy and pharmacology, being specific about the differences between them in terms of the degrees and career prospects. This chapter will also show the importance of these subject areas and their benefits to you and to society, making clear why they are worthwhile.

Chapter 2 will give you an overview of what an undergraduate degree course in pharmacy or pharmacology entails, helping you to make an informed choice on which areas you wish to study and which specific content and structure would suit you best.

Chapter 3 provides a detailed analysis of selecting the course and university which is right for you, enabling you to make an application that not only has a realistic chance of success but will ensure that your experience of undergraduate study is worthwhile. It will consider the entry requirements and the different types of courses in pharmacy and pharmacology and will also focus on the right choice of university at which to study.

Chapter 4 examines the importance of work experience in making the initial choice of undergraduate course and also in strengthening your application and giving you a realistic chance of being offered a place. It will provide guidance as to how to find the right sort of work experience and how to reflect effectively on what has been learned from it.

Chapter 5 is designed to take you through the UCAS application process, guiding you through each stage and helping you to ensure that your completed form is of the highest calibre. It will give you an insight into what the admissions tutors are looking for in successful applications so that they will take you seriously as a prospective student.

Chapter 6 will look at the all-important personal statement and how to make yours really stand out from the rest. It will consider the questions that a personal statement needs to answer, engaging the interest of admissions tutors and providing a basis for an interview. For universities which do not routinely interview, the personal statement gives the admissions tutor an insight into the candidate's understanding of the degree and motivation for studying it, so this chapter will explore how to be really specific in providing this information.

Chapter 7 examines the interview process, making clear what you can expect and the different approaches taken, so that you can be fully prepared. It will give suggestions of specific areas which could be discussed at interview as well as practical tips to enable you to present yourself in the best possible light.

Chapter 8 considers applications which are non-standard, showing how students may come to a degree in pharmacy or pharmacology by different routes. It will cover differences in educational background, such as students who do not have the required subjects at A level or IB, as well as any specific requirements for international or mature students. Students with disabilities and/or special educational needs can also find useful information here.

Chapter 9 will take you through results day and the different scenarios you could potentially face, whether this is having missed the grades required for an offer, not holding an offer or having exceeded the grades required. Recognising the potential for stress on results day, the chapter will enable you to have all the information ready so that you are able to take an informed and clearly thought-out course of action.

Chapter 10 will analyse the fees for courses in pharmacy and pharmacology, providing information for students who are from the UK and EU as well as international students. It will explain the different funding options and any sponsorship and scholarships which are open to you in these subject areas.

Chapter 11 moves beyond the degree courses to explore the different career routes available to students of pharmacy and pharmacology. It will look at typical and alternative career routes and provide information about employment prospects and where graduates with these degrees are to be found. It will also give you an insight into career development and some indication of potential salaries.

Further information will give you useful contacts in terms of websites, organisations and charities as well as literature for further research.

The **Glossary** will define terms that you will meet in the course of reading this book or doing your own independent research.

Recognising the value of drawing on the experiences of current and former students, admissions tutors and professionals who studied pharmacy and pharmacology, the book includes quotations and some full case studies. These case studies give personal insights from a range of individuals and have been selected to develop the information included.

As with the other guides in this series, it is less a definitive exploration of pharmacy as a profession and more of an explanation of the journey towards becoming a pharmacist or working in areas related to pharmacology. Having worked as an adviser to would-be students in a number of sixth forms, I am aware of the pitfalls facing students: choosing the wrong A level subjects, not carrying out or keeping reflective records of work experience and voluntary placements, failing to research and – in many cases – actually visit their chosen universities and assuming they can simply turn up for an interview without thorough preparation. This book seeks to prevent you from falling into these traps and is based on my experience of working with these students and on interviews conducted with those who have taken degrees in these areas.

Pharmacy is a competitive course and students need to do all they can to make their application stand out. The *Which? University* guide (https://university.which.co.uk) shows the percentage of students to whom offers are made, and this ranges from 50% at Aston University through to 87% at Robert Gordon University. However, it is important to recognise many applicants may be deterred from applying to schools of pharmacy that have high entrance requirements. As a result, if these schools have less applicants, offers will be made to a higher proportion of their applicants.The statistics do not indicate how many students took up a place. At Nottingham, for example, in 2016, 1,175 applications were received from the UK, the EU and overseas; the department interviewed about 900 candidates and made offers to about 800 with an intake of 187 in 2016.

Case study: Jessica Thompson, pharmacy graduate

'I thought about having a career in pharmacy from a young age – I am the seventh generation of my family to become a pharmacist, so I guess you could say it is in my blood! Science had always been my favourite subject at school and I knew I wanted to have a profession where I was helping people, but I am far too squeamish for medicine or nursing, so pharmacy seemed the obvious choice! I achieved grades BAA in A level Chemistry, Biology and Psychology, which qualified me for a place on the MPharm degree.

'Before starting my pharmacy degree at Keele University I had done only one week of work experience in a small, independent community pharmacy. I did have a part-time job as a sales assistant, but this was on a non-pharmacy basis. I learned what the role of a community pharmacist actually entailed and the importance of having a good relationship with patients. As an independent pharmacy, it can be difficult to stand out among the bigger chains, but this experience showed me that as long as you have the passion to deliver the best services possible, then you can succeed.

'I graduated from Keele University after receiving my first-class honours degree in pharmacy. I completed my pre-registration training in a hospital and am now undertaking a PhD at Keele University and also locuming as a community pharmacist.

'My favourite part of the pharmacy course was having the opportunity to attend a number of hospital placements as part of the therapeutics module. The role of the pharmacist is changing and the course at Keele reflects this by being more clinically based and integrating learning with practice.

'Keele University is often referred to as "a bubble", due to the campus environment, and as a result there is a very homely feel to it. This is also true for the pharmacy school, and during my studies it was reassuring to know that support from the academic staff was always there. There are always going to be parts of a course that you do not enjoy – for me it was the more chemistry-based aspects of the degree. Industry is a great career option for a pharmacist but it has never been an interest of mine and I found the more analytical side of the degree tough. I am currently completing a PhD at Keele University and I hope in 10 years' time to have had my work published and to be continuing with research. I hope my research gives me the opportunity to travel and I'd love to have a post that involves teaching.'

1 | What are pharmacy and pharmacology?

This chapter is designed to give you a clear insight into pharmacy and pharmacology so that you are able to make an informed choice of degree, understanding what each one equips you to do in terms of further study and careers. Later chapters will go into much more detail with regard to studying these subjects at university and career routes, but this chapter will outline the differences between the two areas and the professions to which they will give you access.

Pharmacy is the study of the management and dispensing of medicines, whereas pharmacology explores medicinal drugs and their effects on the body. It is vitally important to be clear as to the distinctions between these two areas, especially as they sound rather similar! Pharmacy is a demanding degree in terms of the time commitment, in many ways similar to medicine, and will involve time not just in lectures and tutorials but also on hospital wards and on pharmacy placements. Essentially, most students who opt for pharmacy do so because they are looking for employment immediately after qualifying, whereas pharmacology students are more likely to go into research or further academic study on completion of their first degree. Please note that pharmacology is **not** a route into pharmacy and a second degree would need to be taken in pharmacy if a student wished to pursue a career in that area. Pharmacology is offered as a single honours degree and joined with or built on to any of the biomedical disciplines such as genetics or neuroscience.

What can you do with a degree in pharmacy?

A four-year MPharm degree in Pharmacy will enable you to begin a career as a pharmacist. Pharmacy is a profession which is scientific in nature but has a very practical application in terms of a career.

Most of you will have come into contact with a pharmacist when you have been prescribed medicine by a doctor and taken the prescription to be dispensed in a community pharmacy. The pharmacist has the important job of ensuring the right treatment is given out to patients, checking the prescription and referring it back to the doctor if necessary. He or she will also provide advice about how or when to take the medication and is expert in knowing if another prescribed or over-the-counter treatment will interfere with the effectiveness of the medication.

A pharmacist will ensure that there are no errors in dispensing medication, for example that the dosage and quantity of the medication are provided and that the length of time for which the medication needs to be taken is specified. Pharmacists are not allowed to deduce or infer what the doctor has intended but are able to provide advice regarding side-effects and provide support for vulnerable members of society such as the elderly and drug addicts. As they are often the first port of call for people who are concerned about their health and wish to see whether an over-the-counter medication can help them or whether they do need to see their doctor, pharmacists will therefore require to combine scientific knowledge with excellent communication skills.

Pharmacists are not restricted to working in community pharmacies, however. Some work in other settings such as a hospital or primary care, prisons, the army or with organisations such as UNICEF where they will provide support with supplies of medication, or become industrial pharmacists – more detailed information is given in Chapter 11. As a profession, pharmacy does have some aspects in common with medicine and may suit you if you have considered training to be a doctor.

Skills and qualities required for a pharmacist

Students looking to start a degree in pharmacy should enjoy chemistry, with a specific interest in learning more about medicines and the way they impact on the human body. You should enjoy working with and helping people, as pharmacy is a practical, caring profession most commonly based in the local community or hospital. You should have excellent communication skills, a genuine interest in improving people's health and thrive on using your scientific knowledge to solve health-related problems.

As a pharmacist, you will need to be friendly, approachable and keen to continue to develop your knowledge of medicines and their effects. In addition, you should be aware of the ways in which the pharmacist's role is widening to incorporate running health campaigns, following up patients to monitor the effectiveness of their medication and offering advice and referrals to GPs, walk-in centres and hospitals. While a common perception of the pharmacist can be that of a pill counter and dispenser of prescriptions, the role is increasingly wider than this and the capacity to relate effectively to people across all ages and groups in society is essential.

Many pharmacists will go on to run and/or own their business and so will need to develop business acumen to manage stock and accounting, as well as staff. Pharmacies sell a wide range of health and hygiene-related products as well as over-the-counter medications, some of which will be restricted in quantity or only suitable for certain individuals, so a pharmacist will be involved in providing training for counter assistants and helping them to procure any relevant qualifications. The ability to delegate tasks – such as following up medications with patients or preparing prescriptions – while holding overall responsibility for the quality and accuracy of services is an important skill for the pharmacist, so it is essential that you are able to lead a team.

All these skills and the necessary knowledge are acquired during your training, but your academic study and extra-curricular activities, including work experience and voluntary work, will offer an opportunity to demonstrate your potential in these areas.

How to become a pharmacist

The study of pharmacy involves a four-year MPharm degree course followed by a year of practical training, known as the pre-registration year, which leads to approval by the GPhC. The training can take place in any pharmacy environment, as long as you spend at least six months in either the community or hospital sector. This practical experience has to fulfil the guidelines set down by the GPhC to enable the trainee to put into practice the knowledge gained in their master's degree and gain a variety of practical skills which are fundamental to working as a pharmacist. On completion of the pre-registration practical placement, the trainee has to pass the registration assessment in order to gain approval by the GPhC. These assessments are available in June and September each year and consist of two papers that test the trainee's ability to apply their knowledge, make professional judgements and use numerical skills to carry out calculations, all in the pharmacy setting. Trainees are allowed up to three attempts to pass the whole assessment, which must be in the same sitting. Further information about the assessment can be found on the General Pharmaceutical Council website (www.pharmacyregulation.org/education/pharmacist-pre-registration-training-scheme/registration-assessment).

Later chapters will explore the nature of the pre-registration training and the approved settings that will prepare you for working in one of the following areas.

Community pharmacy. These are pharmacies on the high street, either independent or part of a chain, such as Boots, Superdrug and Lloyds. Here you will have a vital role in the National Health Service (NHS) which includes prescribing medicines, reviewing treatments and monitoring how patients take their medicines, as well as dispensing prescriptions. You will be giving direct advice to patients, GPs and other healthcare professionals to make sure that patients take their medicines safely and effectively.

Hospital pharmacy. These are based in hospitals and are responsible for dispensing medication prescribed by the doctors and consultants from the departments across the hospital in a wide variety of disciplines. Pharmacists offer patient-focused care as part of the clinical ward team and will advise consultants, doctors and nurses on the use of medicines.

Primary care. Pharmacists work in GP practices, providing prescribing advice to GPs and nurses, as well as running clinics for patients with long-term conditions. Here pharmacists will use their skills as qualified independent or supplementary prescribers. In primary care trusts, pharmacists will take a major role managing the prescribing budget and giving prescribing advice to GPs and non-medical prescribers.

Pharmaceutical adviser/clinical pharmacist. These pharmacists are involved in primary and secondary care, giving guidance to community and hospital pharmacists in the planning of local pharmacy services.

Research. Your degree in pharmacy will also give you the opportunity to work as an industrial or academic pharmacist.

What is pharmacology?

Pharmacology is the science of drugs and their effect on living systems. A drug is any chemical substance that affects the way our body functions. It can be a medicine, a drug of abuse or a poison. The pharmacologist's job is to understand why taking a pill affects the chemistry of our bodies and to use this knowledge to create more effective drugs.

Pharmacology can be studied with any of the biomedical disciplines, for example genetics or neuroscience. Pharmacology encourages flexible thinking and will appeal to you if you enjoy the possibility of making new discoveries and practical experiments. In your pharmacology degree, you will also study anatomy, biochemistry and immunology as well as the fundamental principles of pharmacology. Some university courses give you the opportunity to study abroad and/or industrial placements. You may be able to get bursaries from organisations, such as BP, to allow you to do these placements and to help with travel and other costs.

Skills and qualities required for pharmacology

A passion for science and aptitude for research are essential for pharmacology, with the ability to work independently on projects, manage time effectively and sustain commitment, since results will not be immediate. Team work is also required, as it is important to be able to communicate well, explaining the process and outcomes of projects to both experts and those with more limited knowledge of the specific area of research.

Attention to detail is vital, as is the ability to set up and monitor experiments with an understanding of ethical guidelines, and to analyse results. An ability to express yourself clearly in writing is also required for composing proposals for research and final reports. While some pharmacologists will be employed in hospitals and university laboratories with set hours which may include weekend and evening work, a flexible approach is needed when meeting deadlines for projects. You may be carrying out research while also lecturing to medical students or those taking either pharmacology or a broader-based science degree with modules in pharmacology, or acting as an adviser to a hospital, so, again, flexibility is required.

What can you do with a degree in pharmacology?

Although graduates of pharmacology are not qualified to work as pharmacists they can be employed in a range of areas, from a pharmaceutical laboratory to a lecture theatre or even a field hospital abroad. You can be employed by the civil service, be called on to give evidence for the legal service or be involved in media consultancy. The scientific skills and knowledge built up in a pharmacology degree are invaluable, not only in their own right, but in the way they develop thinking and creativity.

To improve employability or gain funding for research projects, it is usually necessary to continue in education beyond first degree level, taking a PhD or MRes (Master of Research). Further details on careers are given in Chapter 11, but essentially a pharmacology graduate will work in the following key areas.

Research: Pharmacologists work in laboratories conducting research and working towards new breakthroughs in medicine, a recent example being for a single potent drug to combat high blood pressure which was announced in March 2017.The research discovered the source of nitric oxide, responsible in the body for controlling blood pressure, made by an enzyme influenced by activity in the brain. A new treatment would mimic nitric oxide, possibly through one drug. Given that high blood pressure can lead to a range of serious health conditions, such as vascular dementia, strokes and heart attacks, the implications for this research are wide-ranging.

Teaching: Lecturers in pharmacology can teach either in pharmacology and related departments or in medical schools, preparing future doctors for their careers by covering the clinical pharmacology aspects of their degree.

Clinical pharmacologists will usually have started with a degree in medicine and then gone on to work with patients in hospitals after specialist training. Clinical pharmacologists may be called on to give advice to hospital doctors, consult on a patient who has been poisoned, carry out research or be involved in the university teaching of future health professionals. A lecturer in clinical pharmacology will often have a number of roles, including being involved in clinical toxicology clinics, treating patients in hospital, national advisory work and education. Alternatively, you may be employed in the pharmaceutical industry or be brought in to give advice to patients, scientists, government committees, lawyers or even films and TV dramas to ensure accuracy in the storylines.

The British Pharmacological Society website (www.careersin pharmacology.org) gives a number of case studies of graduates in pharmacology.

Case study: Jasdeep, pharmacy graduate

'I'm currently a pharmacy manager for Boots in Burton, managing 29 members of the pharmacy team. I would say that this is my biggest challenge, as every person is different, with their individual strengths and weaknesses. I thoroughly enjoy my role as a pharmacist because it's what I trained to do. Having gained 10 GCSE qualifications at A* to B grades, I went on to take A level Chemistry, Biology, History and AS Maths, gaining the ABB that I needed to read pharmacy at Aston University for four years. I went on to complete my pre-registration year with Boots.

'I didn't know what I wanted to do as a career when I initially started sixth form. At the end of my first year I spent some time researching courses and I thought pharmacy seemed interesting and paid well! In a typical day, I will check prescriptions against the drugs dispensed by our dispensers for clinical and accuracy checks, give advice to patients who come into the store and carry out services such as flu and travel vaccinations. In addition, I liaise with doctors and nurses to ensure best patient medication outputs. In choosing a pharmacy degree and institution, I found that most schools of pharmacy have similar course structures, so I would advise students to choose one that suits their needs. At the end of the day, they will be a pharmacist. I keep up to date with developments in my profession by being a member of the General Pharmaceutical Council, which releases information on its website very often to keep you up to date. I also read a lot of recent pharmacy journals.

'The advice I wish I had received from a professional while I was at school was to get a job in a pharmacy to broaden my understanding of what is involved prior to making my application for university. I currently have no pre-registration students working with me because I have not been a qualified pharmacist for three years. Interviews are the main way of testing the suitability of students who have completed their MPharm and are looking for their year's placement, along with experience, as it is getting more competitive. The hours are long in pharmacy but I find improving patients' medication compliance to be the most rewarding aspect of my job.'

---

2 | Studying pharmacy and pharmacology

First of all, you will need to submit a UCAS application. It is important to have a clear understanding of this process and of the differences between the ways in which pharmacy and pharmacology are delivered at degree level. A clear grasp of what is required to be successful in a career in pharmacy and the career pathways open to you after graduation in both pharmacy and pharmacology should be identified before you begin your application. The decisions you make now will affect the next three or four years and provide the foundations for a career spanning 40 years, so make sure you do your research!

An undergraduate degree course in pharmacy differs in content and delivery from one in pharmacology and it is important to remember that you need a pharmacology degree will not qualify you to become a pharmacist.

Pharmacy

Pharmacy deals with the practice of preparing, compounding and dispensing drugs for medicinal purposes. The emphasis in the past has been on the development, legal and ethical supply of drugs and their control but added to this nowadays is the focus on counselling and advising patients as well as prescribing. An MPharm course therefore incorporates not only the knowledge but also the practical and communication skills necessary for employment as a pharmacist.

What you need to know about a pharmacy degree

A pharmacy degree takes four years, leading to an MPharm qualification, and entry on to this course requires an A level in Chemistry, with Biology often being the preferred second science, although often Maths, Physics or Psychology are accepted. As the NHS careers website explains, the pharmacy degree course is designed to give students the scientific knowledge and practical skills to become a competent pharmacist. Over the four years, you will develop a professional attitude and responsibility through links that the university will set up with pharmacists and other health professionals. Although the ways in which courses are structured will vary from university to university, they will all cover the following: how medicines work, how people work and how systems work.

How medicines work focuses on the ways in which medicines are used to treat patients (therapeutics), the effects that they have on the patient's body (pharmacology), the ways they are produced, so that you have an understanding of pharmaceutical technology, and the ways they are formulated into the doses needed.

How people work looks at people and populations, covering anatomy and physiology (how the human body works), pathology (the nature of disease and its causes, processes, development and consequences), infection and infectious diseases and wound repair. It will also deal with social and behavioural science and health psychology, and include how to recognise and diagnose, health promotion, disease prevention and drug misuse. Aetiology (the factors which produce or predispose toward a certain disease or disorder) and epidemiology (patterns of health events and health characteristics within populations) are also part of this area of study.

How systems work is concerned with the management of healthcare, how healthcare is regulated and the systems in place to ensure high standards of practice. It includes the organisation of healthcare within Great Britain, public health (the health of a population as a whole) and the professional and legal requirements governing pharmacy practice. It also covers the areas of clinical governance (maintaining and improving quality) and clinical management (working with patients to gain the best possible outcomes from any treatments or care).

On completion of the degree, you will undertake a one-year pre-registration training in order to be qualified as a pharmacist and register with the GPhC. There are 31 universities accredited or provisionally accredited to offer pharmacy degree courses leading to qualification as a pharmacist; the following are those awaiting full accreditation pending visits in 2017/18: five-year integrated MPharm at Keele University and University of East Anglia and four-year MPharm at University of Lincoln, Newcastle University and University of Sussex. Details of the accreditations of all the universities, which have to be updated on a regular basis, can be found on www.pharmacyregulation.org.

After graduation, students can further their education by opting to work towards a doctorate in pharmacy (DPharm) or an MSc in Clinical Pharmacy in Community or Clinical Pharmacy in Hospital. Other post-qualification options include an MSc in Pharmaceutical Services and Medicines Control or an MSc in Pharmaceutical Technology. It is just as important to check the entry requirements for these further qualifications as for the MPharm. For example, a DPharm requires a student to be registered with the GPhC, be a practising pharmacist or pharmacy technician and be working in an organisation that enables them to carry out work-based research and evaluation; they must also have an MPharm and postgraduate pharmacy diploma or a relevant postgraduate master's degree in a relevant subject. Completion of the pre-registration training is therefore required, whereas for the MSc in Pharmaceutical Sciences, this is not the case.

Five-year programmes

Five-year integrated MPharm degrees

Scotland has announced that it will be offering a national integrated five-year degree that includes the pre-registration year. The aim of this new degree programme is to enable students to gain employment immediately after graduation. The new degree will replace the existing four-year degree plus separate pre-registration year and is scheduled to start in 2020 at the following universities:

- Robert Gordon University, Aberdeen
- University of Strathclyde, Glasgow

These universities are in the process of deciding how the workplace learning will fit into the degree timetable and which model to adopt. The workplace learning could be in one 12-month block, similar to the current pre-registration training, or in a series of smaller blocks across the five-year programme. The new structure will need accreditation with the GPhC. If this new degree is approved, the first students enrolling in 2020 will graduate in 2025.

Currently, there are two universities that offer a five-year integrated route to professional qualifications and registration: University of East Anglia (UEA) and University of Nottingham.

University of Nottingham: Pharmacy (with Integrated Pre-Registration Scheme). This model has two six-month pre-registration training periods, one at the beginning of Year 4 and one at the beginning of Year 5, which means that students are registered to practise as soon as they graduate.

University of East Anglia: Pharmacy with a placement year. This model operates in the same way as that of Nottingham. The course started in 2016 and is currently working towards accreditation by the GPhC (General Pharmaceutical Council). Fees are payable for the full five years and the placements are unsalaried.

University of Bradford: Five-year degree option (MPharm practice integrated option). Bradford offers a slightly different five-year degree, and UCAS decsribes it as a sandwich course that includes the pre-registration placement. This model offers two six-month periods of pre-registration training embedded into the degree but not directly supervised by the university. Bradford's website states that graduates leave as qualified pharmacists pending the completion of the GPhC registration examination.

Degrees with integrated pre-registration year for international students

Given the practical difficulties for international students in completing the pre-registration year in the UK following graduation, the University of Bath and Keele University offer a five-year MPharm with integrated pre-registration year exclusively for international students. The pre-registration element of the five-year programme does not pay a salary and tuition fees will be payable to your university for each year of the course.

Students from the UK and EU must check carefully whether any five-year programme is offered only to international students.

Foundation courses

These courses are essentially designed to meet the needs of students who do not have the required entry qualifications to proceed directly to a four- or five-year MPharm degree programme, either because they have not studied appropriate qualifiying science subjects at A level or equivalent, or have not met the standard offer. The details of these courses are provided in Chapter 8, Non-standard applications.

How pharmacy courses are taught and assessed

Pharmacy degree courses combine academic study alongside practical work, with placements and the opportunity to undertake projects. Each course is slightly different, so that you can choose one which appeals to the way you prefer to learn.

For example, the University of Hertfordshire has a strong science base to its course, with interprofessional learning with nurses and therapists, whereas Aston University has close links with hospitals and community pharmacies, GP surgeries and pharmaceutical companies, with an emphasis on professional studies and patient-orientated care. The University of Birmingham incorporates enquiry-based learning, similar in approach to the problem-based learning of some medical schools. Keele University's Active Virtual Environment (KAVE) is used to teach the pharmacology aspects of the course, with 3D characters used to simulate interaction between the learner and a virtual patient or clinical virtual actor (avatar).

At the Medway School of Pharmacy each course includes lectures, seminars, laboratory work, small group work, practice-based activities and assignments. There are also a number of placements throughout the programme, so you will benefit from both academic and practice-related environments.

The basic aspects which will be common to pharmacy courses include lectures, tutorials, time spent in laboratories and conducting experiments, problem-based and/or virtual learning, placements and a research project. Assessment of modules takes place on a continuous basis, for example of practical reports, essays, computer-based exercises, of the research project and by means of end-of-module examinations.

Assessment

Assessment includes written examinations at the end of each year. All courses also have continuous assessment, which contributes the remainder of the overall course mark. Continuous assessments include practical dispensing examinations, structured clinical examinations, presentations (individual and group), written reports, assessment of laboratory notebooks, case studies, essays and multiple-choice questions.

Example of a four-year MPharm degree course: Kingston University

Year 1 introduces the scientific basis of pharmacy, including the study of cell biology, physiology and pharmaceutical and biological chemistry, as well as the importance of naturally sourced medicinal products. Students will gain a clearer understanding of the pharmacy profession and the practical and theoretical aspects of dispensing. They will study important pharmaceutical dosage forms, formulation and manufacturing processes, physicochemical aspects of drug stability and pharmacopoeial and regulatory requirements.

Year 2 focuses on the role of hospital, community and industrial pharmacists. It includes the study of pharmacy law and ethics and good dispensing practice. The science is integrated with the practice, as the interactions between how chemistry, pharmacology and pharmaceutics affect clinical practice are outlined.

Year 3 places an emphasis on body systems and disease statistics. Examples include cancer, its causes, the science behind treatments and clinical management of cancer patients. Opportunities are offered for pharmacy students to learn alongside other future healthcare professionals and to talk to patients about their conditions and treatment.

The main focus in **Year 4** is on the research-based project, for which you will receive tuition in research skills. A problem-based approach is used for more advanced teaching in areas such as pharmaceutical technology and biotechnology. Professional practice topics include advanced prescription analysis, risk management and drug interventions, as well as the wider role of the pharmacist in pharmaceutical care. A total of 20 placement days, mostly in hospital or community pharmacies, are spread throughout the course.

Reproduced with kind permission from Kingston University.

Pharmacology

Pharmacology is a biomedical science involving the study of how drugs affect the human body. As these drugs are chemical agents which will have a strong impact on health, an understanding of biology and chemistry and a desire to study these subjects further at degree level is essential. A typical course will allow you to explore the impact of drugs in the forms of medicines prescribed to treat diseases, poisons and those taken for recreational purposes. Pharmacology explores the way the body deals with drugs, considering the means by which they are taken in and absorbed, how they move within the body, are impacted on by enzymes and whether the body will eventually expel or destroy them. This degree suits students who want a practical approach to training in research methods. As with pharmacy, a degree in pharmacology requires an A level in chemistry, with biology often being the preferred second science, though some universities will accept A levels in maths, physics or psychology instead. If either biology or chemistry is not offered at A level, some universities offer a Foundation course.

Given the range of courses available in this subject area, it is important to research each one carefully to see how they are structured. Where a Joint Honours degree uses the word 'and' to link two subjects, they are usually evenly balanced in their coverage, although students can opt to focus more in one area as they progress. Second subject options are shown in the next section. Where the degree lists the two subjects using the word 'with' there is more emphasis on the first subject, for example 'Pharmacology with Business', 'with Drug Discovery' or, at Manchester, 'with Modern Languages'. Medicinal Chemistry is also offered 'with Pharmacology', indicating that there is greater emphasis on the chemistry. In most pharmacology degrees Year 1 usually takes a broad-based approach, gradually specialising and giving students opportunities to choose options that suit them over the next two or three years. The three-year degree programme at the University of Portsmouth follows this approach, with Year 1 offering a general introduction to university-level education and to the systems of the body and the diseases that affect them, the second an exploration of drug treatments for diseases affecting a broad range of organ systems, while in the final year students will consider future targets for drug discovery and focus on a research project of their choice.

What you need to know about a pharmacology degree

Pharmacology can be studied as a single subject at around 24 universities or in combination with a second subject, such as chemistry, biochemistry, immunology (with an industrial placement), drug discovery, innovative therapeutics (with a year abroad), microbiology, molecular genetics and physiology. Alternatively, pharmacology can be chosen at the end of the first year of a biomedical science degree. At the University of Cambridge and the University of Bath, pharmacology is part of a Natural Sciences degree course and at Cardiff University a degree in medical pharmacology is offered. In Leicester it is offered as Biological Sciences (Physiology with Pharmacology), at Exeter it is offered as Medical Sciences (Pharmacology and Therapeutics, with a professional training year), and at Aberdeen it is offered as Biomedical Sciences (Pharmacology, with an industrial placement). The University of Glasgow offers students on a pharmacology degree the opportunity to study an arts or social sciences subject as part of the first year. A UCAS course search will enable you to research all the degree options currently available for pharmacology so that you can get an idea of the variety available to you, but you must be aware that options within subjects and across a combined degree may be be limited as to the accepted combinations and availability at the time of taking the degree. Degree courses are three- or four-year BSc undergraduate courses (the four-year option including a placement year or year abroad) with London Metropolitan offering a four-year extended degree. Some universities offer an integrated master's degree: MSc (Manchester, Strathclyde, UCL, Wolverhampton), MPharmacology (Bath), MBiol (Leeds, Nottingham Trent), or MSci (Bristol) – these last four years, or, in the case of Bristol which offers a study year abroad, five years. The integrated master's course includes an extensive research project; at Leeds, students have the opportunity to study a range of master's modules, while at Bath students are given greater exposure to research and practical techniques, with all students undertaking a placement in a pharmaceutical company, research institute or university. A number of universities offer the option of a sandwich course, and these include Hertfordshire, Huddersfield, Kingston, Leeds, Nottingham Trent (BSc or MBiol) and King's College, London. Hertfordshire and Liverpool have the option of a year abroad.

While the integrated master's degrees develop research skills beyond those of a bachelor's degree, many students continue their education by studying for a PhD, an MRes or British Pharmacological Society (BPS) diploma, but the lateral, scientific skills that they learn within a pharmacology degree make graduates attractive to a wide range of employers.

How pharmacology courses are taught and assessed

Pharmacology is taught by means of lectures and practical, laboratory-based work, along with tutorials, workshops, computer-aided learning and a research project which allows students to gain experience in a chosen subject area, for example pharmacogenomics or neurodegenerative diseases. Some universities will support students in gaining work placements, often in the summer break, while sandwich courses allow for a year's placement. Some modules give opportunities for field trips. The amount of time spent studying pharmacology where it is chosen as part of a Joint Honours course, or where modules in pharmacology are offered within a broader science degree, varies from university to university and details are available on their websites. Assessment of modules takes place on a continuous basis, for example of practical reports, essays, computer-based exercises and the research project and by means of end-of-module examinations.

Example of a BSc Pharmacology course: University of Leeds

The information in this course outline was correct in June 2017, but as is the case with all degree courses, the options for pharmacology may change over time in line with ongoing developments. The undergraduate programme handbook available on the website (www.fbs.leeds.ac.uk) shows the most up-to-date information, and students interested in applying for this course are encouraged to contact the department if they have any specific queries regarding the modules and, in particular, the availability of optional modules.

Year 1 provides the necessary background in physiology, neuroscience and anatomy to understand how the body works. Students are taught the principles of pharmacology which are essential for understanding how to treat disease. Lectures are complemented by practical sessions to provide the skills relevant to pharmacology.

Year 2 focuses on the drug treatments used for various diseases, including cardiovascular and brain disorders. More advanced practical classes develop students' pharmacological experimental skills, covering areas such as chemotherapy and toxicology.

Year 3 uses all the knowledge and expertise students have developed over the first two years to study advanced topics in pharmacology. Students undertake their own research project, covering a cutting-edge topic working under the supervision of a leading expert.

Students are required to study 120 credits in each year.

Year 1

Compulsory modules

- Basic Laboratory and Scientific Skills (20 credits)
- Foundations of Biomedical Sciences (40 credits)
- Biology of the Mind (10 credits)
- Introduction to Pharmacology (10 credits)
- Basic Laboratory and Scientific Skills 2 (20 credits)
- Human Endocrinology (10 credits).

Optional modules (students may study 10 credits):

- Career and Professional Development for Life Scientists (10 credits)
- How can Biological Sciences change the world (10 credits)
- Life in the Extreme: Ultra Human Physiology (10 credits)
- Introduction to Microbiology (10 credits).

Discovery modules (students may study 10 credits of discovery modules).

Year 2

Compulsory modules:

- Cardio-respiratory Physiology and Pharmacology (20 credits)
- Experimental Skills (10 credits)
- Scientific Skills (10 credits)
- Neuropharmacology (10 credits)
- Principles of Drug Discovery (10 credits)
- Experimental Skills in Pharmacology (10 credits)
- Topics in Pharmacology (10 credits).

Optional modules (students must take ONE of the following):

- Neurobiology
- Cognitive Neuroscience: The process underlying cognition
- Sensory and Motor Neuroscience.

Additional modules (students are normally required to take a minimum of 10 credits from the following):

- Chemotherapy (10 credits)
- Introduction to Toxicology (10 credits)
- Physiology of Absorption and Excretion (10 credits)
- Molecular Neuroscience (10 credits).

Discovery modules (students may study up to 10 credits of discovery modules agreed by the programme leader).

If a further 10 credits are still required, students may take a discovery module OR one of the following:

- Employment, Career Planning and Professional Development for Life Scientists (10 credits)
- Skills in Communicating Research beyond the University (10 credits).

Year 3

Compulsory modules:

- Advanced Scientific Skills (20 credits)
- Advanced Topics in Pharmacology II (20 credits)
- Research Project in Biomedical Sciences (40 credits)

Optional modules (students are required to study 20 credits from one of the following):

- Integrative Biomedical Sciences (20 credits)
- Advanced Topics in Pharmacology I (20 credits).

Additional modules (students are required to study 20 credits from the following):

- Inherited Disorders (10 credits)
- Cellular Cardiology (10 credits)
- Systems Neurophysiology (10 credits)
- Drug Development: Pre-Clinical to Practice (10 credits).

Reproduced with kind permission from the University of Leeds.

Pharmaceutical science

Pharmaceutical science focuses on the design and development of new drugs for clinical purposes. The degree deals with exploring where medicines come from, how they work and how they are formulated, analysed and tested. This course provides a wide understanding of all aspects of the pharmaceutical industry and prepares graduates for further study (master's and postgraduate) or for work in a variety of industrial settings.

Degrees in pharmaceutical sciences at some universities have the option of a year abroad, a placement and a Foundation year. At Keele University, pharmaceutical science is combined with technology and business, while at other universities it is possible to study pharmaceutical chemistry, chemistry and pharmaceutical science, or pharmaceutical science with medicinal science and – at De Montfort University – pharmaceutical science with cosmetic science.

3 | Choosing your course

In this chapter we will look at making the right choice of course, in pharmacy or pharmacology, and finding the university for you. Making sure that you can meet the entry requirements and knowing how to research effectively will ensure that you are successful in your application and are undertaking a course which prepares you for your chosen career.

Entry requirements

Before you look at specific universities, you need to check carefully the entry requirements for pharmacy or pharmacology to ensure that your application will be taken seriously and that you have a good chance of being accepted for your chosen course. Use the UCAS course search and check university websites on a regular basis, as requirements can change according to the level of demand for a specific course. Chapter 8, Non-standard applications, deals with routes which are not covered here, such as Foundation programmes leading to the full degree, and there is advice in Chapter 9, Results day, as to how to proceed if you do not meet the offers you have been made. For now, we will look at the standard requirements.

Understanding what is needed at an early stage in your education, preferably before you embark on A level study, will ensure that you have taken the subjects required. Discovering that you need an A level in chemistry at the point of making an application or even halfway through the AS stage will mean that you either have to rethink your degree or restart your A level course to meet the requirements. While some schools do not offer all students the opportunity to take separate sciences at GCSE you should not be deterred from taking biology, chemistry or physics at A level if your background is in GCSE Double Award Science or Science with Additional Science. Offers will stipulate the number of sciences required and those which are preferred, usually chemistry and biology, and there is no specific premium for studying arts subjects to demonstrate diversity.

For a four- or five-year MPharm, the preferred A level or Scottish Highers combination is chemistry with at least one other science subject, usually biology although many universities will accept mathematics.

Most universities do not accept general studies and/or critical thinking as part of an offer. Offers for students taking A level qualifications are usually made in terms of grades and these range from AAB to BBB, with ABB being the average. The new points-based Tariff system reflects the lower value of AS examinations in the new system; whereas they formed 50% of the legacy qualifications, most subjects are now reformed (mathematics being a notable exception as this will be examined under the new system for the first time in 2019) and the AS does not form part of the A level. Where students have taken an AS in a subject for which they do not take an A level, the points allocation is 40% of the A level qualification.

Qualification and Grade	Tariff from September 2017 entry onwards
A level grade A*	56
A level grade A	48
A level grade B	40
A level grade C	32
A level grade D	24
A level grade E	16

Table 1: UCAS Tariff conversion chart

Where a university such as Portsmouth makes offers in terms of Tariff points, it will stipulate the points required in specific subjects. For 2018, these are a minimum of 32 (Grade C) points in chemistry and either biology or mathematics, with a total requirement of 128 points.

For pharmacology degrees, A level Biology or Chemistry is the minimum requirement. Two sciences are required at A level, but these can include mathematics, physics and sometimes psychology and geography. Offers are generally a little lower than for pharmacy – which does not necessarily reflect any difference in the academic demands or quality of the course, but the generally more competitive nature of applying for pharmacy. Offers for pharmacology generally range from ABB to BBC, but universities may be more flexible on results day with students who have not quite met the offer. Again, it is important to check the specific requirements of each university.

Changes to grading in GCSE qualifications

In 2017, the reformed specifications in English language and mathematics GCSEs moved to an award of Level 1 to 9 rather than the legacy grading A* to G. Science and many other subjects will also be awarded by levels in 2018, but these changes affect only England and not Wales and Northern Ireland where the old grading system will continue. The chart given by Ofqual to show how the levels approximate to grades is available on their website (www.gov.uk/government/uploads/system/uploads/attachment_data/file/638308/Grading_new_GCSEs_from_2017.pdf) and is as follows:

Levels 7–9: A to A*

Levels 4–6: C to B

Levels 1–3: G to D

Level 4 is considered as equivalent to a low C and awarded to the bottom third of students who would have achieved C in the legacy qualification. The upper two-thirds are expected to gain a 5. The lower third of students achieving a B in the legacy qualification will gain a level 5 with the upper two-thirds gaining a 6. As a consequence of there not being direct correlation of a single level with the old grading system, where universities use levels in their entry requirements, there is some inconsistency as to whether a 4 or 5 is needed instead of a C and a 5 or 6 for a B. All universities show grades, regardless of whether they also stipulate levels, to accommodate students who took a qualification pre-2017 or one that is still operating under the grading system. This is the case in Wales and Northern Ireland, and with qualifications such as the CIE IGCSE which offers international and independent schools the choice of either a specification with A* to G or Levels 9 to 1. Edexcel IGCSE, available to independent and international schools, are to change from grades to levels in 2018.

For pharmacy and pharmacology degree courses, all universities will continue to require, as a minimum, C grade or its level equivalent in English and mathematics, and most still state this in their entry requirements information as a grade rather than a level. As level 4 is considered as a low C, a level 5 would be more secure. Some universities will require the equivalent of a B grade in English language and/or mathematics. Given below are examples of the requirements of a selection of universities to show the variation in the way they are linking grades with levels for their MPharm degree:

- Birmingham: B/5 in mathematics and C/4 in English language.
- UEA, Brighton, Hertfordshire and Nottingham: B/5 in mathematics and English language.
- Huddersfield: C/5 in mathematics and English language.
- Keele: B/6 in mathematics and C/4 in English language.
- King's College, London: B/6 in mathematics and English language.

It is vital to check the most up-to-date GCSE requirements of each university via their website and to make contact with the admissions department if in any doubt. Applicants must be aware that it is not only A levels (or their equivalent) which are assessed by universities when making offers.

Choosing your course

As has been emphasised elsewhere, the fundamental difference that you need to be aware of in choosing whether to study a pharmacy or a pharmacology degree is that only the MPharm course qualifies you to practise as a pharmacist. It is usually four years, with some universities offering a five-year course including the compulsory one-year pre-registration course which completes the qualification.

For pharmacology, BSc, MSc and MSci courses are available, a BSc being undertaken at undergraduate level and leading to a bachelor of science Honours degree, usually lasting three years unless it includes a placement year or year abroad, and the MSc and MSci leading to a Master in Sciences qualification. The MSc and MSci differ in that the former is taken after an undergraduate degree, whereas the latter combines the bachelor's and master's degrees in one integrated package. Both involve the writing of a master's thesis.

At University College London, for example, the first three years of the course are the same for the BSc and the MSci, but in the fourth year the MSci students undertake an Advanced Laboratory Research Project and can choose from other optional modules. Having completed a BSc in Pharmacology or a related area, you can opt to undertake further study at master's or PhD level, and this is a common route for students wishing to pursue a career in research, where further study is required.

Choosing your university

Once you have made a decision as to which course you intend to study, the next significant choice is where to study. While the availability of your chosen course may impose some limitations on your choice of university, other factors need to be taken into account. Before starting your research or booking time to visit universities, it is good to draw up a list of factors that are important to you. These can include the following.

* **The geographical location.** How far it is from home and the cost/ length of time to travel; the distance of accommodation (halls of residence and off-campus accommodation) from the lecture halls; facilities (social, sporting, etc.) and shops.
* **Cost of tuition fees, accommodation and living.** As well as the scholarships and bursaries available, students at London universities are eligible for a larger maintenance loan, since costs are higher in the capital city. Outside London there are considerable regional differences in the cost of living and accommodation.
* **The choice and availability of halls of residence.** Many offer both catered and self-catered accommodation and the decision as to which is most suited to you will depend on your confidence in

budgeting and cooking. The availability of en suite accommodation, kitchens, flats or individual rooms and size of rooms are other factors to consider. You should also enquire as to when and how you can apply for rooms and the likelihood of getting your first choice.

* **Availability of part-time employment.** Opportunities can be available through the university, for example in the student union bars, but you may also wish to investigate the local area for work in retail and bars/restaurants.

* **Course structure.** Researching the ways in which the course at each university is structured will enable you to see what flexibility and range of options are open to you in each year of the course. The way the course is assessed and the balance between ongoing assessment (termly exams/coursework and projects) and end-of-year examinations will affect your decision. When visiting the university, it is also advisable to find out about the teaching style and whether it fits the way you learn.

* **League tables and statistics.** There are many surveys and sources of data that can be used to judge the quality of universities and specific departments and these use a range of criteria. These sources include: Unistats and NSS (National Student Survey), *Which? University Guide*, *The Complete University Guide*, *The Times* and the *Guardian* and the QS global ranking of universities. In 2016, the Teaching Excellence Framework introduced a scheme that judged universities on the quality of their teaching, awarding gold, silver and bronze to participating universities. These judgements are made on the university as a whole, rather than on specific departments, and the award given is shown on the individual university page on the UCAS site. In 2017, the scheme was voluntary but the majority of universities opted to take part.

There are a number of very useful sources of information which you can use to research universities, which include the following.

* **UCAS course search (www.ucas.com).** This site provides a wealth of information and is continually being upgraded to make it as user friendly as possible. It allows you to search by course and then shows you all the relevant information for each university delivering the degree programme. It is also possible to search by university and then to see all the courses available at that institution. UCAS course search will give you a breakdown of the entry requirements and an overview of the course, details of the relevant departments and links directly to the university website.

* **University websites.** Each university has its own website, details of which can be found either via a search engine such as Google or from the UCAS course search. Although universities do still publish prospectuses, the online versions are more commonly used these days than hard copies. It is important to remember that universities use their websites and prospectuses as marketing tools, each

wishing to recruit the best students, and so they will be presenting their courses, accommodation, facilities and support for undergraduates in the best possible light.

- **Visiting the universities** to which you intend to apply is vital. General open days are advertised on the website and information will be sent to your school or college. Many universities also invite students to post-offer open days, which are geared more specifically to the course and are aimed exclusively at students who will be making their firm and insurance decisions. Some universities use invitations to open days as part of their application process and an opportunity to informally assess applicants, but I would suggest that you view any time visiting a university in this light, as well as your chance to really be certain that it is the right place for you.
- **The Student Room (www.thestudentroom.co.uk)** has forums which allow students to exchange information about their experiences of applying to university, of courses and careers. While you can gain a great deal from talking to students when you visit a university, student ambassadors are likely to give a rather biased view, as they will have volunteered and sometimes are paid for their help on open days.
- *HEAP 2018: University Degree Course Offers* is published annually as an independent guide showcasing the range of degree courses available and their entry requirements. In addition to the published text, there is an online version (www.heaponline.co.uk) which will have the most up-to-date information, since you will find that universities do sometimes change their requirements to suit the popularity of a specific course or requirements of a profession.

Overall, as the case study below indicates, it is important to enjoy what you do and to be motivated to succeed. While many students, like Ruth (see Case study, pages 29–30), may choose a course as an alternative to their original goal, having the right entry qualifications and experience as well as the personal skills and qualities will enable you to be successful in your degree and future career.

MPharm courses accredited by the General Pharmaceutical Council (GPhC)

- Aston University (Birmingham)
- University of Bath
- University of Birmingham
- University of Bradford**
- University of Brighton
- Cardiff University
- University of Central Lancashire (Preston)
- University College London
- De Montfort University (Leicester)

- Durham University
- University of East Anglia* (Norwich)
- University of Hertfordshire (Hatfield)
- University of Huddersfield
- Keele University
- King's College, University of London
- Kingston University London
- University of Lincoln (provisionally accredited)
- Liverpool John Moores University
- Medway School of Pharmacy, Universities of Greenwich and Kent
- University of Manchester
- Newcastle University (provisionally accredited)
- University of Nottingham*
- University of Portsmouth
- Queen's University Belfast
- University of Reading
- Robert Gordon University (Aberdeen)
- University of Strathclyde (Glasgow)
- University of Sunderland
- University of Sussex (provisionally accredited)
- University of Ulster (Coleraine)
- University of Wolverhampton

Providers with one asterisk next to them offer a five-year integrated degree and those with two asterisks offer a five-year sandwich course. All MPharm degree courses are provisionally accredited while the provider is working towards full accreditation. Accreditation is reviewed by the GPhC, usually after five years, and the accreditation reports for each university are available via a link on their website.

The following MPharm degrees are accredited by the Pharmaceutical Society for Northern Ireland:

- Trinity College, Dublin
- Royal College of Surgeons of Northern Ireland
- University College, Cork

The degree course offered by University of Ulster has dual accreditation from the GPhC and by the Pharmaceutical Society for Northern Ireland.

Case study: Ruth, pharmacy graduate

'For me, pharmacy was an alternative career to medicine and one that I certainly don't regret. As I initially wanted to study medicine, my work experiences were related to medicine. The work experiences were at GP surgeries and a hospital in London. This work experience also helped me prepare for pharmacy as well, as I was privileged to interact with some pharmacists. From my work experience, I learned about the administrative aspect of things, information governance and patient care, i.e. making patients the priority. I also learned a lot about team work. In my A levels I gained ABB in maths, biology and chemistry, and two Bs in AS level Psychology and Physics.

'I enjoyed studying pharmacy. It was very interesting, interactive and practical. From the outset, I knew I didn't want a career that was just bound to laboratories, so I chose pharmacy rather than pharmacology. The course allows for patient contact, which is important to me. However, it is a lot of work – you have to be on top of things, be organised and are constantly busy.

'I have just finished my pre-registration year and, looking back at university, it definitely prepared me for the real world. My only issue is that I feel that the intensity of the course should be made known to students beforehand. This is because most people arrive and they get the shock of their life! With courses like medicine, this is expected because you are made aware of that through the various selection processes and requirements. But I feel that with pharmacy, most people don't expect the level of intensity that the course actually entails. I enjoyed the group work, when it is not assessed; the place-ment, as it allowed us to put what we learn into practice; and modules on pharmacy practice, law and ethics, which gave us insights into the day-to-day issues surrounding the profession.

'I see myself as a doctoral degree holder researching into pharma-ceutical issues, making contributions towards professional development and the improvement of patient care. In addition to that, I will also ensure that I am in touch with the core of what pharmacy is about, which is engaging with patients and other members of the healthcare team. I will do this by attending conferences, seminars and workshops where current or pressing pharmaceutical issues are deliberated. In choosing your course, I would advise the following.

- Speak to current university students.
- Make a list of things that are important to you, then use this to choose your universities – not the other way round. On this list must be the course content and how good the course is. After visiting the universities, cut this down to two or three, then rethink, based on everything, to choose the final one.
- Be realistic about your choice, based on your performance, but at the same time don't limit yourself. You have five choices, so choose wisely.
- Don't follow friends – follow your heart.'

Case study: Jennifer Powley

Jennifer is a pre-registration pharmacist at Derby Teaching Hospitals NHS Foundation Trust.

Why did you choose to study pharmacy?

'I chose to study pharmacy because, for me, it was the perfect balance between patient care and science. From a young age I had always enjoyed science, particularly chemistry. Pharmacy is a degree where you get to put all of your chemistry knowledge into practice, and then being able to apply that knowledge to a patient and their care is something I find fascinating. The pharmacist has a unique role to play in the care of a patient as the specialist in medicines, and this apect of the job has always appealed to me.'

How did studying MPharm Pharmacy at Aston help you to achieve your current career position?

'My time at Aston provided me with the vital experience that I needed to apply for a pre-registration position in a hospital pharmacy. Throughout the four years of the course I was able to undertake placements in a number of different hospitals, which gave me a good feel of the role of a pharmacist in hospital. This enabled me to understand how the pharmacist can really make a difference in the hospital setting and gave me an insight into the key skills that are needed by a hospital pharmacist.

'The degree at Aston provided me with a deep-seated understanding of clinical knowledge combined with formulation knowledge, which is vital when undertaking the daily tasks of a pharmacist. In addition, throughout the degree I was also repeatedly exposed to situations where I could test this knowledge, be it during lectures, workshops or placements. This enabled me to push myself and develop my understanding further, and gave me the essential skills that I could discuss during my pre-registration application and interviews to show that I was an ideal candidate for a position in the hospital sector.

'Finally, and perhaps most importantly, the degree at Aston gave me a passion for pharmacy and the value of the pharmacist in a hospital. I was able to convey this when applying for a pre-registration place and I strongly believe that it helped me achieve a pre-registration place in hospital.'

What are your future career goals?

'Pharmacy can provide such a wide and varying career. At the end of my pre-registration year, I intend to return to university to complete a PhD in drug formulation development. I also plan to continue developing my clinical practice working in the hospital sector, with an aim to eventually lecturing on an MPharm degree programme in the future.'

What advice would you give students considering studying pharmacy?
'For any students who are considering studying pharmacy, I would say "DO IT!". Pharmacy is a unique career with a range of future career opportunities, including within the community, hospitals and industry. It is a career where you are constantly learning and developing your skills. The role of the pharmacist is continually evolving, with openings for independent prescribers, specialist pharmacists and pharmacists in GP surgeries, to name just a few. The opportunities for a pharmacist are well and truly endless.'

4| Work experience

Live to work or work to live?

In making your choice of career, only you can ultimately decide what is important to you. This may be job satisfaction, status, salary, the opportunity to continue to learn and develop, flexibility or a combination of some of these. Undertaking a degree, pre-registration placement (pharmacy) and progressing through different stages of a pharmacy- or pharmacology-related career will be academically challenging, so it is important that you make an informed decision.

Relevant work experience is therefore crucial in the decision-making process and is just as valid in confirming your interest in either pharmacy or pharmacology or in making it evident that it is really not the right route for you. At its best, it will show you what a career using these degrees can lead to, whether your skills and qualities equip you for these options and whether you will gain satisfaction from pursuing it.

For an admissions tutor in pharmacy, the work experience you undertake and your ability to reflect upon it in the course of your personal statement and – where relevant – your interview, will be an important part of their decision as to whether to offer you a place. In an increasingly competitive academic field, evidence of work experience demonstrates your initiative and commitment to the subject, your understanding of what is involved and how far your skills and qualities are suited to the degree. If you are unable to arrange a placement by the time you make your application, you must show through your personal statement that you understand what the role of a pharmacist involves and how you are suited to it.

> 'We assess personal statements for the applicant's commitment to pharmacy and whether they really know what the subject and career entails. Work experience or paid employment in a pharmacy is a good way of gaining this understanding.'
>
> Ian Smith, Admissions Tutor at Keele University

> 'We are looking for applicants who show a genuine interest in the course and in working in the industry.'
>
> Lee Buttery, Admissions Tutor at Nottingham's School of Pharmacy

Both Keele and Nottingham universities will consider candidates with interests in healthcare who might be applying for other courses as a first choice, such as medicine, since they will possess many of the same interests and skills. Work experience may also include placements in hospitals, GP surgeries and care homes.

Pharmacy

The first stage in finding out what is involved in being a pharmacist is to seek out as many opportunities as you can to talk to pharmacists who are working in different locations. Probably the easiest of these is your local community pharmacist, since they can be found in high street pharmacies or within major supermarkets, many of which offer services from early in the morning to late at night. Pharmacies are also attached to doctors' surgeries and operate the same opening hours. Talking to a pharmacist about what makes their job both rewarding and challenging as a career and finding out what initially drew them to this career and whether it has fulfilled their expectations is a good start to your research. Although you are unlikely to be very formal in your approach, it is sensible to make a list of the questions you want to ask and encourage the pharmacist to offer you advice as to the best way to gain practical experience.

From this initial meeting and conversation, you may be able to undertake a period of work shadowing where you watch the pharmacist at work, preparing medicines to be dispensed from prescriptions, answering queries raised at the counter by customers or counter staff or having private consultations with customers about their prescriptions and their suitability/side-effects. A minimum of one week, either as a block or over several sessions, would be a sufficient amount of time to demonstrate to an admissions tutor that you have been able to gain an adequate insight into the profession, and it is better, where possible, to do this in more than one location – an inner-city pharmacy will present different challenges from a rural pharmacy. Pharmacies increasingly offer a range of services beyond simply selling and dispensing medicines, so the opportunity to see the pharmacist carrying out meetings with patients to check that they are correctly taking their medication or tests for diabetes, high blood pressure and cholesterol and to support healthy eating and stopping smoking will all help you to see the breadth of the profession today.

Gaining experience in a hospital or industrial pharmacy is likely to be more difficult, unless you have some specific contacts, but it is worth contacting your local hospital and writing to pharmaceutical firms.

A number of students I have worked with have been able to gain part-time paid employment working in pharmacies as counter assistants and this has not only given them the opportunity to see the day-to-day work of a pharmacist, but also given them an insight into the nature of community pharmacy and the different demands made on pharmacists by customers. Some students have also completed a Pharmacy Counter Service course, learning about the guidelines relating to dispensing prescriptions and selling over-the-counter medication.

Pharmacology

If you are interested in a career as a research pharmacologist or clinical pharmacologist, the BPS suggests that you start by talking to patients of Parkinson's, ADHD, cancer, etc., whose conditions are managed by medication. This will give you an understanding of the effect certain medication has had on their lives, in terms of both the improvements to their quality of life and the side-effects it causes. You may have a relative who has taken medication or may be able to talk to carers in homes for the elderly or the residents themselves. The BPS can also be a source of information about higher education establishments which may allow you to experience research or teaching in pharmacology.

If you are interested in a career as a clinical pharmacologist, the best starting point would be to contact universities which employ senior lecturers in clinical pharmacology. As well as being involved in the teaching of medical students, they are usually employed to give advice to hospitals in cases such as poisoning, and may be happy for you to shadow them and find out more about their work.

Work experience relevant for studying pharmacy and becoming a pharmacist will also give you useful insight into pharmacology. You will be able to see drugs being dispensed and find out about their impact on the human body through spending time in a pharmacy.

Arranging your work experience placement

Many schools and colleges provide support with organising work experience, especially during the GCSE years, and may well have placements which they have established over a number of years. If not, your careers department, tutors or head of year should be able to offer guidance in locating relevant placements and practical help with writing letters, making telephone calls and the logistics of attending work experience.

It is important that your work experience is recent and relevant, so it would be advisable to use the holiday time in the first year of sixth form to undertake any extra or first-time work experience so that it is fresh in your mind, ready for making your university application between September and January of the final A level year. At this stage it is likely that you will need to find your own placement and make your arrangements; being able to say that you have done this independently will be more impressive on your personal statement and when discussing your experience at interview.

Using any contacts that you have, such as through family, friends or simply calling in to your local community pharmacy are good ways of identifying possible placements. Alternatively, you can make use of the internet or Yellow Pages telephone directory (www.yell.com).

Guidance from an admissions tutor about work experience

Simon Tweddell, Director of Admissions at Bradford University sees work experience as important in assessing a student's application. He says, 'We would look at students' motivation and commitment to studying pharmacy and becoming a healthcare professional. We would be looking at their experiences to identify what transferable skills they might have developed, for example from work experience, voluntary, charity work, caring responsibilities and/or activities such as Duke of Edinburgh Awards or National Citizen Service, etc, and sports, hobbies or pastimes that might have developed their skills to work in a team and solve problems.

'In the interview, we would look for the student to 'demonstrate that they can discuss their experiences with us and show that they possess values congruent with those of a future healthcare professional, the ability to work with others and to reflect on their experiences and to relate them to those of a caring healthcare professional. Whether it is through a pharmacy placement or other experiences, we would expect them to show some understanding of current pharmacy practice such as examples of what a pharmacist does from day to day and their role in preventing illness.'

Writing a letter of application for work experience

Your letter needs to be clearly and accurately written, giving some details about yourself and your reasons for undertaking the work experience at the pharmacy. The style should be formal and include details of a referee, usually someone who knows you well from school or college. Your form tutor, head of year or careers tutor would be well placed to act as a referee for you. Ring the pharmacy to find out the name of the person to whom the letter should be addressed.

An example of a letter is given in the box opposite.

27 Royal Walk
Edgbaston
B22 3DP

Mr P. Jones
Edgbaston Pharmacy
Main Street
B20 3NR

21 April 2017

Dear Mr Jones,

I am currently studying in the Sixth Form at Edgbaston Community College and interested in pursuing a degree and career in pharmacy. My A level subjects include chemistry and biology, giving me the required scientific background, and I am keen to undertake some relevant work experience to give me more insight into the profession. I would very much appreciate an opportunity to initially meet with you to discuss the role of a pharmacist and to arrange, if possible, to shadow you and the counter staff to gain some first-hand experience.

My personal tutor, Mrs Sally Cooper, is happy to provide a reference for me and can be contacted as follows:

Mrs Sally Cooper
Edgbaston Community College
High Street
Birmingham
B22 3DF

Her email is sally.cooper@edgbaston.community.co.uk and her direct line is 0121 454 9888.

I am available from 4pm each day and at the weekends for times to suit you. I would be grateful if you could contact me at my home or school address, by email (james.brown@hotmail.co.uk) or telephone (0121 454 9777) to discuss my request further.

I look forward to hearing from you.

Yours sincerely,

James Brown

How to take full advantage of your work experience

Having set up the placement, you need to ensure that you are able to use the experience to:

* discover whether this is the right career route for you
* gain knowledge and understanding which will be relevant to your personal statement
* prepare for questions in a university interview.

It is therefore crucial that you prepare for the experience effectively and take time to reflect on it and what you have learned. Prior to the first day, write down what you hope to do, what you want to discover and any specific questions which you want to ask. This will help to structure the experience more efficiently. These questions could include:

* what a typical day in a pharmacy (or pharmacology placement) involves
* the challenges of the role and for other members of the team, for example the counter assistants, and how they work together
* the training and experiences the pharmacist (or clinical pharmacologist) has had
* the pay, career and further training opportunities, hours of work and alternative routes available in the profession
* what your colleagues like and dislike about their role
* the qualities required for their role and advice they would give to someone embarking on this profession.

Keeping a record of what you have seen and discussed in your placement, with some very specific examples and your thoughts and feelings about them, will enable you to convince an admissions tutor of your understanding of the profession and your suitability for it. Keeping a jotter or notebook with you to record what you have seen and the answers to questions you have asked will ensure that your memories of the experience are clear when it comes to the personal statement and interview.

Taking a professional approach to the placement

A pharmacy- or pharmacology-related placement is a professional environment and it is crucial that you take the right approach. This approach begins with how you present yourself, wearing smart, clean clothes similar to those worn by the pharmacist, clinical pharmacologist or others working in the same environment. You will be coming into contact with members of the public in the pharmacy and therefore need to project the same image as the regular staff so that they are happy to have you there. Being polite and relatively formal in the way you communicate with staff and members of the public, again taking your cue from those around you, will ensure that you feel comfortable in the placement and have the opportunity to ask for a reference, which could be incorporated into your UCAS application. If you have not had a part-time job or are unused to this type of communication, discuss it with your tutor at school or college and practise meeting and greeting people.

What you will do in your work experience placement

The opportunities open to you will vary according to the placement and the willingness of the employer. You may simply be shadowing or be given some practical jobs to do; whatever these are, be ready to offer to help in whatever ways you can, however mundane. In a pharmacy, this could involve learning to serve customers and do the first stage of processing a prescription, organising stock and drugs as they are delivered, tidying displays and cleaning, and all of these will give you a keen insight into the business side of running a pharmacy. Many pharmacists today own their own business or are managers of a branch in a large organisation such as Boots or one of the major supermarkets, and so the skills of business management are required in addition to professional knowledge as a pharmacist. You will also see that being a pharmacist goes beyond simple dispensing of prescriptions and see the variety of customers who will come for advice and health checks.

In a pharmacology-related placement, such as a university laboratory, you are likely to have the opportunity not only to sit in on lectures and seminars, but to also observe practical experiments and discuss ongoing research with research pharmacologists. If you are lucky enough to spend time with a clinical pharmacologist, he or she could be working in a number of roles in a working week and so you may be able to attend hospital, see them lecturing university students in the School of Medicine or even advise on a patient who has been poisoned through, for example, an overdose.

Being observant: what to look out for in your placement

Consider what each member of the team does on a daily basis and take time to talk to them about their training and career plans. For example, in a pharmacy, in addition to the pharmacist, there will be the counter assistants, who are in the front line of communication with customers.

You will be able to observe and ask them about the variety of customers and queries they deal with and the guidelines they need to abide by in terms of selling over-the-counter medications as well as when they need to refer the customer to the pharmacist. You will also be able to find out about the increasing opportunities for counter assistants to train in taking blood pressure and carrying out health checks as well as following up customers on long-term medication.

Take time to observe the pharmacist in their interactions with customers to see the type of queries they deal with – ranging from side-effects of prescribed medication, supporting elderly patients and drug addicts with medication, to suitability of over-the-counter products. In many ways, pharmacists are becoming a first point of call for people who may discuss health concerns before deciding whether to see their doctor, and noting how they deal with sensitive queries and how they create this relationship will give you more insight into the job. Make sure that you keep a note of any specific technical terms relevant to the medications, treatments or advice given.

Reflecting on your placement

Take time to consolidate and reflect on the notes you have made in the course of your placement and to consider whether you still want to make an application for pharmacy or pharmacology. Hopefully, the placement will have given you an insight into one specific aspect; you may then wish to find another in a different area, for example a hospital pharmacy, and all of this will demonstrate the strength of your commitment to an admissions tutor as well as ensuring that you feel certain of your choice of course.

> At the end of the placement, remember to thank your employer. A letter or card will ensure that you leave a positive impression and keep the door open for any future requests. This would also be a good opportunity to request a brief reference from them.

Voluntary work

Developing the personal qualities required for pharmacy and pharmacology is as important as having an insight into the profession and there are many ways in which voluntary work can help you to do so. These qualities are in many ways similar to those of healthcare professions such as dentistry and medicine and include a concern for the welfare of others and a desire to make a practical difference to their lives. You need to show that you can work with a variety of people in contexts which take you beyond those of home and school/college. Working for a charity in a fundraising shop, day care centre or home, helping at youth clubs or after-school clubs, special schools, sports centre or holiday clubs or looking after an elderly relative or neighbour can all develop your skills and, most importantly, confidence. Sustaining a commitment will show your integrity and genuine desire to help others, so this should be either for at least two weeks in a block or a regular weekly commitment for six months or more. Students taking the Duke of Edinburgh's Award qualification will be able to incorporate this experience into their Service section, whereas training in first aid could be used for the Skills section and taking this award at Bronze, Silver or Gold is another way of demonstrating relevant personal qualities. As with the work experience, keeping notes of what you have seen and done will be beneficial for the application process.

Paid employment

Having a part-time job can be beneficial in a number of ways, whether or not it is directly related to pharmacy or pharmacology. For a student, opportunities are more readily available in retail or hospitality such as a local supermarket, fashion store or cafe and restaurant. Even a straightforward job such as a paper round will demonstrate your ability to sustain a commitment and to be punctual and reliable. Jobs involving working directly with members of the public will enhance your communication skills and give you experience of working under pressure.

While you need to be careful about how much time you take away from your academic study, a part-time job can reflect your ability to manage your time effectively and create a work–life balance. A reference from an employer can be given to whoever is writing your UCAS reference and positive comments can be used to support statements about your personal skills and qualities.

Case study: Qam, pharmacy undergraduate

'Up until I was 18 I always thought I'd go into law or accounting. It wasn't until my uncle told me about a possible pharmacy work experience placement at Modi Pharmacy in Halesowen that I became interested in pharmaceuticals. I really enjoyed the practical nature of the tasks I was given. It is important to me to work in a job that makes a difference and I know pharmacy will enable me to fulfil this ambition. The variety of careers related to pharmacy is more than you'd think. I want to work in a team in a hospital. Although my work experience showed me how enjoyable the practical side of dispensing medicine is, it also showed me how isolated community pharmacists can be. Getting a job as a pharmacist in a hospital is hard, which is motivating me to be the best I possibly can at university.

'Work experience is the best thing. It not only gives you an authentic experience of pharmacy, but universities want to hear that you have the experience. I worked once a week at Russells Hall Hospital in Dudley, which inspired me to work in a hospital environment. I also worked at Acorns Hospice in Birmingham, where I looked after the patients in an empathetic way, whereas at Russells Hall Hospital I was involved in administration. Both placements gave me ongoing insight into the medical world and helped me write a detailed personal statement. I would encourage anyone to try out different work experience, even if it is not directly pharmacy related. It's a real eye-opener.

'My work experience and ambition to study pharmacy inspired me to do well in my academic work. In my GCSEs I achieved six A grades in science, English language, English literature, religious studies and Urdu. I got an A* in ICT and a B grade in maths as well as reaching Level 3 in my Key Skills course. I had to work extremely hard in my A Levels and I achieved A grades in biology and chemistry and a B grade in accounting.

'There is a huge difference between sixth form study and university. The main one for me is that there is no specification to follow. The university writes its own programme of study, which you have to stay on top of, as there isn't a website like AQA that you can refer to. You need to be organised. I sit down and rewrite my notes after every lecture. This helps me cement what I've learned as well as produce neat revision notes. The number of modules each year is much higher too. I studied six modules this year.

'I am in university from 9am to 4pm Monday to Friday. The week is split into lectures and practical work. We complete two practicals a week that are each four hours long. We have 12 lecturers, who are experts in specific areas of pharmacy. They deliver the lectures and are keen to chat to us about any difficulties we're having with the subject. The level of support is really good, however, in looking back I realise I was a bit spoiled at my sixth-form college in having small class sizes and so much time with my tutors. It's different at degree level, where you're part of a big student community and need to be more independent and self-motivated.

'This year I will be focusing on physiology as Year 2 is all related to Medicine Discovery, which I'm really excited about as I love studying the human body. In Year 3 – Pharmacist as Practitioner – we will be focusing on the patient, and then in Year 4 – Application of Pharmacy Knowledge and Skills – I will be writing my dissertation. My favourite sessions are the compounding practicals. It is in these sessions that we create dry medicines such as paracetamol. I am a member of the RPS (Royal Pharmaceutical Society) and the GPhC. The RPS is more relevant to students, whereas the GPhC supports new pharmacists beginning their career. Both have excellent websites that display news on developments in the industry.

'I'm enjoying studying at De Montfort University and living in private accommodation. It's been good living in a new place and the social life is good in Leicester. I don't party really, but I'm part of the Bollywood Society and play for the pharmacy football team.

'Ultimately, I want to work as a pharmacist in a hospital. Working face to face with patients who need medicine is what I want to do. It's a job that makes a difference. I am interested in community and industry pharmacy, as there are obvious similarities. I really want to feel part of a pharmacy team and it's the hospital area of pharmacy that offers me this.'

5 | The UCAS application process

In order to apply for your chosen course you will need to complete the application form on the UCAS (Universities and Colleges Admissions Service) website (www.ucas.com). UCAS deals with around 2.5 million applications each year for around 650,000 courses and is the organisation which processes your form, submitting it to each of your university choices for consideration and recording their decision on your application.

The UCAS site has a wealth of information on how to make your application, track your offers and respond to them and how to go through UCAS Extra, Clearing and Adjustment as necessary. It contains videos of different stages of the application process and has help boxes alongside the different questions on the form to support you in filling it in. As the application process is online, you can fill in the form anywhere that you have access to the internet and can save as you go along. Schools and colleges usually run higher education preparation days and will often organise visits to universities where advice about the application process is given. UCAS organises Higher Education Conventions all over the country where representatives of universities and colleges will give advice specific to their course and there are generic talks on the application process and specific ones for vocational and highly competitive courses.

To register for UCAS, you will need to have an email address and to have decided whether you are applying through your school or college or as an independent applicant. Applying through your school or college will enable it to check your form as you fill it in, approve it and verify your qualifications and then, once it is all completed, add the reference and predicted grades for the examinations you have yet to take. You will be given a school or college buzzword to enter in the registration stage and should ask your head of careers/year for it. It is only when the reference has been added that the form will be forwarded by your school or college to UCAS, who will send it to your chosen universities. Mature students, international students and those applying after their A level results will usually fall into the category of independent applicants.

Once you have registered, you will be issued with a username and password, which you must store safely; your school or college will not have these details on file, so if you lose them you would need to contact the UCAS helpline to access them. UCAS will allocate a personal identification number, which needs to be quoted in any contact with it or your chosen universities.

The application timeline

As with any major undertaking in life, planning ahead and being aware of the deadlines is crucial to success with your application, particularly in competitive courses. Although neither pharmacy nor pharmacology specifically requires a 15 October deadline, as is the case for medicine, dentistry and veterinary science, this early deadline does apply if you intend to apply to Cambridge for pharmacology as part of its Natural Sciences degree. Further information about applications for Cambridge can be found in another book in this series, *Getting into Oxford and Cambridge*. The standard deadline of 15 January for ensuring fair and equal consideration of all applications is relevant for all other universities, but the sooner you can send your application, the better, since many will start to give offers without waiting for the deadline.

Late applications will be accepted up until 30 June and international students may be given more leeway, but equal consideration cannot be guaranteed. After 30 June, applications are accepted by UCAS but will not be forwarded to universities and students will be eligible for Clearing instead. The message is to apply as soon as you can, since your application is more likely to get the careful attention of the admissions tutor if it is not landing on their desk with hundreds of others, as can be the case as the January deadline approaches.

The timeline below provides an overview of the different tasks you will need to complete over the course of a typical two-year A level course but it can be adapted to suit other programmes of study.

Year 12

September: By now you should have gained some relevant work experience or undertaken voluntary work, which we discussed in Chapter 4. If not, now is definitely the time to begin so that you can show commitment over a period of time before you submit your application next September. Use contacts and be pro-active to gain experience over weekends and holidays. Begin researching courses and universities and look out for open days.

October: Begin visiting universities and colleges by attending open days.

June/July: Schools and colleges will be encouraging you to do your serious research, including attending open days at the colleges and universities that appeal to you. You can also arrange to attend the UCAS Higher Education Convention closest to you, either through your school or college or independently via the UCAS website. Collate information about your courses and create a shortlist. The UCAS site will go live for applications for places the following year at the end of June and you will be able to register and begin filling in your form.

August: Research alternative student-written and departmental brochures/prospectuses and read league tables and Student Room forums (www.thestudentroom.co.uk). Sign up for any open days in September/October or ring to request individual visits for any universities you are considering but have not yet seen. Draft your personal statement.

Year 13

September: Complete your UCAS form online and submit it as soon as possible. It will be accepted from 1 September. Remember that your school or college will need up to two weeks to approve your form and attach the reference, so allow plenty of time for an early application.

15 October: Deadline for applying for pharmacology as part of Natural Sciences at Cambridge.

November: Universities will hold further open days, sometimes as part of their admissions process, and interview prospective students. Offers will start to be made.

15 January: Deadline for all other UCAS applications.

February/March: Offers and, sadly, rejections will have been notified. UCAS Extra is available for students who are not holding any offers either because they have been rejected by all their choices or have decided to withdraw from any of them and decline offers. UCAS Course Search will indicate which courses still have places available and you can apply for these, one at a time. Some universities will hold open days specifically targeted at students to whom they have made offers and this will help you to decide which offers to accept.

April/May: The deadline for accepting offers is usually 7 May, but this will vary according to when you have received your final offer or rejection, and so may be different from other students whom you know. You will select one firm and one insurance choice. You will need to fill out applications for student finance and Disabled Students' Allowance if applicable, involving your parents/guardians, and many universities will allow you to apply for accommodation, especially at your firm choice.

May/June: Sit your exams and await results. The final date on which late applications can be sent to a chosen university is 30 June, after which such applications are automatically entered into Clearing.

July: International Baccalaureate results released 5 July. The last date for adding an Extra choice for 2018 entry is 4 July. Clearing vacancies are listed in the UCAS search tool from the beginning of July.

August: Scottish Highers results released at the beginning of the month (7 August in 2018); A level results the penultimate Thursday of the month (23 August in 2018). UCAS Track is updated to confirm offers at firm or insurance choice universities on results day and Clearing/ Adjustment goes live. Universities will wait until 31 August for results and you should let them know if there are any which will be delayed. Universities may make you an offer of an alternative course or of a deferred place. Once you have gained a place, you will confirm your acceptance and finalise accommodation.

The ten stages of the application process

1. Registration

The registration process sets you up with a UCAS account for the current application cycle. Registration is available from June, but UCAS applications can only be submitted from 6 September for courses starting the following September/October, although it is possible to apply for a deferred place.

The basic identification information given at this stage, such as your name, address, date of birth and email address, will be transferred to the Personal Details section so that you do not have to repeat it. You will be prompted to identify whether you are applying as an independent candidate or as part of your school or college; for the second option, you will need to enter the name of the institution through which you are applying and the system will then have this on record. For a large educational institution, you may also be asked to identify the tutor group or teacher that is overseeing your application and will provide the reference.

The username allocated to you is made up of your first initial, surname and a number, for example njones4, and you will provide your own password, which you must note somewhere for future reference. Once you have completed the relevant sections you will be sent an email to verify your account; the email will contain a verification code which you need to enter on the system. At this stage you are registered to complete an application and will be allocated a personal identification number, which you must also record safely.

Once you have registered successfully with UCAS and received your registration details you can begin filling out your UCAS application (but not submit before 6 September). As you fill in each of the sections detailed below, make sure that you always save your updates before you move on or log off, or all your hard work will be lost. A dotted line will appear next to the relevant section on the left-hand side of the screen to show that you are working on it. Once you have finished a particular section, you can click at the bottom of the page to indicate it is completed and it will then have a tick on the left-hand side. Your school or college UCAS adviser and referee will be able to check how far you have progressed with your form, first by accessing a list which will show the sections started and/or completed and then by accessing your individual form.

2. Personal details

The information used for registration will be transferred to your online application form, but this section requires more detailed information about you, such as your nationality and whether you are resident in the UK. International students will need to complete details of their passport, as will any students who were not born in the UK. It is worth noting that you need to be very careful in your response to the Criminal Convictions section, especially for pharmacy, where the nature of any conviction could preclude you from working in this profession, and tick it only if you do have a conviction to declare.

Remember that before you submit your application, you will be asked to declare that all the information on the form is accurate and that you understand that any inaccuracies can lead to your application being cancelled and offers rescinded. If you are in any doubt about this, or any other section, talk to your school or college adviser or ring the UCAS helpline (0371 4680468).

3. Additional information

In this section you are asked about any specific courses you have attended in preparation for your application and you are advised to list ones which are directly relevant in terms of the skills, knowledge or understanding of the degree. Information about your background, such as whether you have been in care and your parents' education and employment, will be used for statistical purposes and will not impact on the outcome of your application. Completing the Student Finance section and allowing UCAS and universities to share information with the Students Loan Company (www.gov.uk/student-finance) will not only ensure that you are prompted to make the application for funding but will remove the need to provide all the personal information already on your UCAS form and allow details of your final offer to be provided so that funding goes to the right place. University grants and bursaries will be made directly available to you if you qualify by reason of parental income, or your own income if you are independent of parents or guardians, so it is very helpful to allow sharing of information for this purpose.

4. Choices

In this section you are able to apply for **five** courses and it is possible to put together a combination of pharmacy, pharmacology and/or pharmacology-related courses, or even any of these with a different course entirely. Remember that the one personal statement has to be used for all the courses and that you need to make it relevant, so it may be better for you to leave other course applications as options for UCAS Extra or Clearing. Pharmacy and pharmacology can also be the fifth choice for an application for early-deadline subjects such as medicine, dentistry or veterinary science where only four places can be chosen. Universities will not be able to see which other choices you have put on the form.

The form will prompt you for the institution code which identifies the university, the course code, site on which you will be studying (usually the main site), start date (which will be the next academic year unless you are making a deferred entry) and the point of entry (required only if you are joining in the second or later year of the course). You will also be asked to indicate whether or not you will be living at home to attend the course. All of these sections have drop-down or help tabs to enable you to access the required information. The choices will appear on your form in alphabetical order for the universities and will be sent to all of them at the same time, so you are not indicating any order of personal preference. If you have originally applied to fewer than five institutions, you can add further choices, as long as you do so within the deadlines.

> You do not have to apply for five courses and I have known students who are particularly committed to one university, or whose personal circumstances make it impossible to apply anywhere else, to put only one choice.

5. Education

Before you begin to fill in this section, find all your relevant certificates and statements of results so that you have the required details of the qualifications, examination boards, dates and grades achieved to hand. Remember that you and your school/college will be asked to confirm that these achieved qualifications are accurate, so don't be tempted to make any changes!

UCAS will have access to the results of any new qualifications before you receive them in August and it is on the basis of the grades achieved that your offer will be confirmed or rejected. It is therefore of the utmost importance that you do not just enter the details of qualifications which you have taken, including ones which you have failed, but also those you are currently studying and for which you are anticipating results. You will be asked to indicate the highest level of qualification that you expect to achieve before embarking on the course for which you are applying, and this is usually 'Below Honours degree level', unless you are taking a second degree.

Predicted grades will be given by your referee for any qualifications that are pending and these will be influential in terms of the university's decision to make you an offer. If you do not have any pending qualifications, the offer will be based on the grades you have already achieved and so the offer you receive will be unconditional.

Some universities will make conditional offers based on Tariff points achieved at A level, where an A* gives 56, A is 48, B is 40, C is 32, D 24, E 16 and an AS level carries 40% of the number, as long as it is in a subject not taken at A level. Your offer may state that the points have to be taken from a certain number of full A levels, for example 120 points from three A levels, in which case any subjects taken only to AS level are not included in your offer but may have been taken into account in deciding to make an offer to you because of the breadth of study or relevant skills/knowledge they represent. The offer in points may also have a reference to a specific grade requirement in one or more subjects, for example 120 points including an A grade in chemistry. With the reformed A level system, fewer students are taking AS examinations and universities will not discriminate against students who do not take them, especially where this is the school/college policy.

The strength of your academic record and predicted grades form the basis of any conditional offers or interview invitations made to you, so it is imperative that you take your time to make sure everything is recorded correctly.

6. Employment

Have you had a part-time or full-time job? If you have been employed, whether this has been over a holiday, in the evenings or weekends, it will show that you are responsible, reliable, committed and that someone has been willing to pay you! There may be directly transferable skills relevant to pharmacy, such as working in retail or with customers in a cafe or restaurant or actually in a pharmacy itself. Equally, you may have done data entry or worked in a job requiring practical skills relevant for both pharmacy and pharmacology. The details required are very simple: name of the employer and nature of the employment, together with the dates and whether it was full or part time. You should include only paid work in this section and will have the opportunity to refer to work experience and voluntary positions in your personal statement. If your employer wishes to contribute to your reference, you can arrange for them to send details to the person in your school or college responsible for its completion.

7. Personal statement

It is advisable to work on this in Microsoft Word or another word processing program before transferring it to the space allocated in the personal statement section of the form. You have only 30 minutes in any one time you are logged in to the system, so you may be in danger of losing anything you have written if you work directly in UCAS. Drafting your statement in Word will also allow you to use spellcheck and other proofreading tools, which will help you to identify any mistakes in spelling, punctuation and grammar but should not be wholly relied upon.

The space available for your personal statement is 47 lines and 4,000 characters, including spaces, but you may find that what started out in Word as fitting within these limitations is slightly over or under on the UCAS form. When you have copied and pasted your statement onto the form, you need to click 'Preview' to check that it fits. Anything over the limit will not show. Preview will tell you how many lines and spaces, if any, you have left over.

We look at the personal statement in more detail in Chapter 6.

8. View all details

At any stage in the completion of the form, you can click on this section and see the whole form as one document. Accessing this feature will give you an overview of how far you have progressed, but it is most useful when all the sections are showing as complete. This is the point at which it is crucial to check every detail thoroughly and it can be helpful to leave time between filling in the sections and doing this checking so that you can come to it with a fresh eye. Asking friends, family, a relevant professional or your school or college to do this with you will ensure greater accuracy. Once you have checked this section, you will again click to indicate that it is completed and will then have access to the final section for which you are responsible: Pay and send.

9. Pay and send

Once you click to access this section, you will first be directed to read and agree to a number of statements which focus on the accuracy of the information; your acceptance of the rules governing UCAS applications; and state that you are happy for UCAS to share details of your application with the universities to which you have applied and with your school/college or anyone else responsible for your reference. In agreeing with these statements you are effectively entering into a formal, legal contract with UCAS. After you have ticked the relevant boxes, you will be asked how you want to pay and have the option of credit/debit card and – if applying via school or college – a cheque directly from your centre, which may then invoice you. The cost is £12 for an application that uses just one of the five choices allowed and £23 for two or more.

Having filled in the pay details, you will then see a message telling you that your form has been sent, usually to your school or college, and this enables the reference to be attached. It is important to realise that the form has not yet been submitted to UCAS, but remains to be checked by your school or college, which can return it to you via UCAS if it spots any errors to be corrected or additions to be made, together with an email explaining what and why. If this is the case, you simply resend once you have made the necessary amendments. Once this stage is completed, the reference will be added. The process is slightly different for independent candidates, who will be given the opportunity to request a reference via the UCAS application system rather than this being done at the Pay and send stage.

10. Reference

The quality of your reference and the predicted grades, coupled with your previous academic record and personal statement, will play a large part in the decision made by any of your chosen universities to make you an offer. Universities want committed students who possess the motivation for the course and your referee needs to be able to reflect that you have these qualities in the reference that they provide. The reference will be written by someone from your school or college who knows you very well and who will collate the comments of teaching staff in your academic subjects together with those relating to extra-curricular activities, positions of responsibility and work experience. The referee will normally be your head of year, personal tutor or head of careers but the reference will have been initially drafted by the person who knows you best. You need to ensure that they are familiar with experiences you have outside school and are fully aware of your desire to study pharmacy or pharmacology.

The personal statement and reference should work together as a representation of you and your commitment to the course, showing how and why you are suitable for it. For the admissions tutors, the referee's view of your skills, knowledge and personal qualities will be of great value. They will also be able to explain any extenuating circumstances which may have impacted on your examination performance to date or may do so in the final session, such as health, family circumstances and change of schools. It is advisable to discuss the content of your reference and predicted grades before you reach the stage of submitting your form and many schools and colleges will allow you to see it before it is added. Once the reference has been completed, together with the grades for any pending qualifications, your application will then be sent to UCAS.

After your application has been submitted

You will receive notification by text and/or email to confirm that your form has been submitted. There is no system for making trial applications but you have seven days to notify UCAS of any changes to your choice of courses/universities, after which time you need to go directly to the relevant university to see if they will accept them. If they will accept the changes, the universities concerned will advise UCAS on your behalf.

Accepting firm and insurance choices

Once all the universities have responded to you, offering you either a conditional place, unconditional place (if you are applying with your grades already achieved) or rejection, you then need to decide which to accept. You are allowed to accept two offers, one as your firm choice and the other as an insurance, so it makes sense that your insurance choice, wherever possible, has lower grade or UCAS points requirements. Your firm choice is your preferred university and course, but it is important to point out that you are making a contract with the universities by accepting both choices and that if you are unsuccessful with your firm choice, but meet the requirements for your insurance, you are expected to take up this place. As no university is really going to drag you kicking and screaming – to speak metaphorically – to its course, it will usually release you if you have changed your mind, but this can delay applying through Clearing for other places.

UCAS Extra

As can be seen from the timeline at the beginning of this chapter, there is a facility for making additional applications if you do not receive any offers or decide to reject the ones you have. UCAS Extra gives students the opportunity to apply for some excellent courses without having to wait until Clearing. The system allows you to apply for several courses in Extra, but only one course at a time.

If you have applied for pharmacy, but have not received offers, you could consider a university with a Foundation course, especially if your predicted grades have led to rejection. With both pharmacy and pharmacology, if you originally applied for high-demand courses, you could consider related or alternative subjects, or a joint degree course. However, it is important to remember that only an MPharm degree will enable you to qualify as a pharmacist.

You can make some changes to your personal statement through Extra if this would be more relevant to the additional application and support it more effectively. Pharmacy and, to some extent, pharmacology, has been seen as a potential Extra choice for students who applied for medicine and were rejected by all of their four choices. The Extra process runs from 25 February to 4 July in 2018 and dates will be very similar in following years. Use the UCAS search tool at www.ucas.com to find out which courses are advertising vacancies in Extra and make contact with the relevant university or college to see whether it would consider you before making your application through Extra.

UCAS Adjustment

If you have achieved better grades than the ones required for your firmly accepted offer, then you will be given up to five calendar days from the time that your original place was confirmed (or A level results day, whichever is the later) to make some changes as to where and what you wish to study. It is up to you to put yourself forward to be considered for Adjustment; if you do so, then you should contact the relevant university and admissions tutor for confirmation that it both has places available and will consider you. The period for Adjustment ends on 31 August. While you are making an application through Adjustment, your original offer is held for you so that you will not lose out. Some students may use this service to apply for the same course at a university which requires higher grades, or may apply for either pharmacy or pharmacology for the first time, especially if they have gained grades which were higher than expected.

Deferred entry

You can make a deferred entry at the time of submitting your application, for example to start your course in 2019 when applying in the 2018 cycle. This enables you to have a gap year, certain in the knowledge that a place awaits you. The university will be interested in any plans that you have, and will be keen to see you doing something valuable in this time. You could gain employment in a related field or where you will develop relevant skills, take additional qualifications or travel. Voluntary work in the UK or abroad will enhance your profile. The other way to defer your place is to contact the university once they have made you an offer or even once you have your results. It is not guaranteed that they will be prepared to hold your place to the following year. The disadvantage to a deferral can be that a student may lose focus on their academic studies, however this is usually outweighed by the benefits. It is important to ask the university early in the process how they feel about a gap year as each admissions tutor will have a different policy and may be less flexible with a competitive course such as pharmacy.

University admissions tests

Although these are not always immediately obvious on the university websites, a number of pharmacy schools use IOT (Institution's Own Test) either online prior to interview or as part of the interview process. UCL and Portsmouth have online tests, and the website for Portsmouth states it will test knowledge of biology, chemistry and mathematics along with English and situational judgement (at interview). UCL does not have specific details on their website but feedback from students who took the IOT there in 2017 indicates that it includes mathematics, ethical scenarios and an essay on a health-related issue. Candidates are not expected to have A level Mathematics but to have good GCSE-level mathematical skills. The admissions test for Liverpool John Moores University is taken on the same day as the interview and tests understanding of the qualities required to be a pharmacist, and skills in mathematics and comprehension.

Admissions tests are used in conjunction with each university's other selection criteria, such as predicted grades, education profile to date and performance in the interview.

Spotlight on Cambridge: Pharmacology through BA (Hons) Natural Sciences

Application procedure

The initial application is submitted through UCAS by the early deadline of 15 October. Students opt either to apply for one specific college or for an open application, which means that they can be interviewed by any college interested in them. Once the UCAS form is sent, it is immediately followed by the Supplementary Application Questionnaire that provides further information to the chosen college about the student and their areas of specific interest in Natural Sciences.

The next stage of the application procedure is the pre-interview written assessment for Natural Sciences – the NSAA (Natural Sciences Admissions Assessment) – and this is taken at a local centre, usually the applicant's own school or college. There are specimen papers available on the University of Cambridge website. The NSAA consists of the following sections:

Section 1: Maths and science MCQs (multiple-choice questions) – 80 minutes

Section 2: Science-specific longer questions – 40 minutes

The NSAA is aimed at the high-performing students, predicted A and A* grades, who will be choosing Cambridge, and is intended to be intellectually very demanding. Even very able students will score about half marks on average. Performance on the NSAA is used alongside the personal statement, reference, prior performance and predicted grades to determine whether an applicant is invited for interview.

Magdalene and Trinity colleges set an additional written assessment as part of the interview process.

Mature students who are applying to a mature college are not required to take the NSAA, but will take a common format written assessment at the interview, if invited to attend on the strength of their application.

The interview

Cambridge receives five applications for each place per year and approximately 75% of applicants are interviewed. Offers are only made to those who attend an interview. Normally one in four applicants is pooled (referred for consideration by other colleges than the one to which they originally applied) and – of these – one in four receives an offer of a place from a college other than the one for which they applied or were allocated. In 2016, this was 853 students, accounting for 20% of all the offers made.

Cambridge does not recommend applicants to pay for courses that prepare them for interview; they provide advice via a YouTube clip on their website. Research via the internet also yields sample interview questions (www.cambridgeinterviewquestions.com/questions/sciences/natural-sciences and www.oxbridgeapplications.com).

In addition, there is a sample Natural Sciences interview recorded by Emmanuel College (www.emma.cam.ac.uk/admissions/video/interviews/?showvid=98) that gives an idea of the nature of questions.

The interviews are designed to show what candidates know and understand, but also how they can apply their existing knowledge and skills to unfamiliar scenarios. They will be asked questions beyond the scope of their A level specifications and given problems to work through in order to test their thinking processes and how they are likely to respond to the nature of teaching at Cambridge.

General tips on the UCAS application

- Be organised in your research.
- Register as soon as the system goes live in June. You can begin filling in the application form, but won't be able to submit it before 6 September.
- Remember that the admissions tutors are looking for potential and a genuine desire to study the course, coupled with the appropriate A levels or equivalent.
- Print out a copy of your completed form and make sure you get it checked before you send it off.
- Check your emails and Track regularly to ensure that you respond to any offers of interviews or online questions sent to you by the universities.
- Reply to offers by the deadline.

Final advice from a university graduate

'It is important to stand out when completing an application form – just make sure it is not for the wrong reasons. *Always* check your spelling and grammar, because competition is tough and it could make the difference between securing an interview and not. Secondly, if you are finding it tough to write a personal statement it may be helpful to have somebody else write a list of what attributes they think you possess; it can be difficult to think objectively about yourself.

'When it comes to work experience, it is always handy to have some in pharmacy – not only does it look good on your application form but it can help to determine if it is the right career for you. However, any work experience is good experience, as you can translate many skills that you have learned into any work environment. Throughout the pharmacy degree I would advise on getting as much pharmacy experience as possible, especially in the sector in which you are most interested in working; this will increase the likelihood of getting the pre-registration place you want. It can be difficult to get hospital and industrial placements but it is important to not give up – get out into the pharmacy world and network! A brilliant way to do this is by signing up for and attending events put on by the British Pharmaceutical Students' Association (BPSA) and the Royal Pharmaceutical Society. The BPSA played a huge role in my pharmacy journey and I would highly recommend getting involved to improve your future prospects. My overall advice to those wishing to study pharmacy is: *be prepared, be calm, be yourself!'*

6 | Personal statement

This section of the application form is important enough to be given a whole chapter to itself and is the most demanding of all the sections. Let us begin by deciding on its purpose.

The personal statement gives the admissions tutor an insight into the reasons why you want to study the course and your suitability for it. It should show your motivation, commitment and what you have done to prepare yourself – academically and personally – for the application and what qualities and skills you possess. The key to the statement comes in the word 'personal' and although you can have advice as to how to plan and structure it, with guidance as to the areas to cover, no one else can write it for you. Universities will use software to detect plagiarism and they want to find out about you, so it must come from you. The statement has to fit within the space allocated, which is 4,000 characters including spaces, and 47 lines in Times New Roman font 12.

How to begin

There are various ways to prepare for this, and getting the relevant experience and academic qualifications is explained in other chapters. Now you have to plan what you will write.

Start by creating a list, flow chart or mindmap and include:

- your academic studies: what you have enjoyed, the skills and knowledge gained and additional reading and research to supplement and extend your A level study
- extended projects, experiments and lectures you have attended
- work experience, voluntary work and paid jobs
- hobbies and interests
- travel
- positions of responsibility
- achievements in sport, music, drama and activities such as CCF (Combined Cadet Force) and Duke of Edinburgh's Award
- carer responsibilities and support you have given to others
- any defining moments that have led to this application.

As you write, give specific focus to what you have learned and the qualities you have developed through each of the above so that it will not read as just a list when you come to write it in extended prose. It is important to be really specific, so note down examples of what you have done.

Once you are happy with your first draft, be prepared to ask for advice from your school or college, where your tutor, head of year or careers or one of your A level tutors will have plenty of experience in giving feedback. You can also involve friends and family members who know you well – they will be able to tell you about skills and qualities they know you possess or remind you of particular experiences. While you do not want to come across as arrogant, you do need to 'sell yourself' and people close to you can help in this regard.

There is no excuse for a personal statement riddled with technical and grammatical errors, badly structured or incoherent – the spelling and grammar check on your computer can identify many of the problems, but asking several people to proofread it for you will ensure it makes sense! However, remember that though you may get a variety of different responses on the content, in the end, it is **your** statement and you are likely to talk about it at interview.

As we discuss in Chapter 7, Interviews, it is important that – like the rest of the form – you can verify that the content is accurate and you should avoid exaggerating an experience or making claims about research and wider reading that you cannot support. The case of the 'stick insect expert' who claimed to be passionate about such creatures and to have extensive experience of breeding and reading about them is a case in point. Intrigued by this statement and keen to know more, the admissions tutor invited a member of his department who was indeed such an expert to be on the interview panel. Sadly for the student, his expertise extended only as far as keeping one at the age of seven and it had been his unfortunate mother who had done the 'looking after'. Needless to say, the interview did not proceed very well after this point and an offer was not made!

University admissions tutors are keen to discover what makes you interested in pharmacy or pharmacology and want to know about your experiences to date which have led to your application. Work experience, voluntary work and evidence of some of the NHS Six C Values (Care, Competence, Commitment, Courage, Compassion and Communication) would be relevant to pharmacy. Some of these will also be relevant to pharmacology, but for pharmacology more of an emphasis on intellectual interest in science would be expected. Avoid clichéd statements or material copied from sample personal statements or those used by a friend, however successful these may have been!

> 'In the personal statement we look for a strong commitment to healthcare practice and an interest in pharmacy (drawing on academic experiences and transferable skills). The personal statement is important for pharmacy due to the clinical nature of the programme and the profession the programme leads onto.'

> Thomas Matthes-Buck, Admissions Tutor at
> Aston University's School of Pharmacy

Structuring a personal statement

The personal statement must be relevant to the course. For pharmacology, it must show clearly that you have the scientific background knowledge, interest and potential to undertake a degree which will lead you into research or practical applications in this area. You need to relish the opportunity to develop your study of chemistry and biology, with a good level of mathematics. In discussing your A levels, wider reading and work experience, this passion must be evident. You may also signal possible career routes from this subject. Use broader interests, such as sport, music and drama, and positions of responsibility to highlight personal qualities which are relevant to the course and/or potential career, rather than simply presenting them as a list. It is likely that for a degree in pharmacology the balance will be two-thirds academic and work experience and one third broader interests and responsibilities. Please note that for pharmacology at the University of Cambridge, as part of its Natural Sciences course, the personal statement will need to be more heavily weighted towards the academic side with a maximum of 20% focused on extra-curricular activities and interests.

The following are examples of personal statements, with comments as to their quality and – where relevant – how they could be improved.

Personal statement for pharmacology

Academic areas of the personal statement: why pharmacology?

The personal statement should focus on your interest in the subject you are applying for, in this case demonstrating your passion for pharmacology. You should make this the main focus of your personal statement and try to be as creative as possible in demonstrating how you have explored the subject both inside and outside of school.

First draft

My interest in pharmacology is closely linked to my interest in biology at A level. By studying the ways in which cells and organs work I have come to understand what causes biological systems to fail and how these occurrences can be prevented. Pharmacology will enable me to learn about drugs and their effects on the body, with the chance to study anatomy, biochemistry, immunology, genetics and neuroscience.

Within biology I have studied antibiotics and have been particularly fascinated with the topic of resistance. My time at a community pharmacy showed me how many antibiotics are used within medicine and the reliance we have on them. I was interested in the way the pharmacist advised customers. Studying A level Chemistry has allowed me to work upon my practical skills, allowing me to evaluate results and draw conclusions. Experimental work highlighted the key link between chemistry and pharmacology. Together with maths, I have been able to develop my problem-solving abilities, which I feel will aid my learning at university.

My work experience reinforced my underlying interest in pharmacology. Having spent two weeks at a local community pharmacy I saw how the role of a pharmacist has developed to not only dispense drugs but advise on them. I was fortunate to spend time in a laboratory at my local university, seeing how experiments over a long period of time are needed to understand the side-effects of drugs and how a breakthrough will come after years of research.

Comments

Areas of academic study relevant to pharmacology have been identified and the student begins to give some examples, but is tending towards generalisations, for example the comments about practical work in chemistry. The final sentence in the opening paragraph is simply a statement of what is studied on the degree course and is not linked to why the student wants to study pharmacology.

The comments on the work experience could imply that the student is more drawn towards pharmacy, and so the scientific interest in drugs and the desire to pursue this needs to be more evident.

Final draft

My interest in pharmacology is closely linked to my interest in the study of cellular and molecular areas of biology at A level. By studying the ways in which cells and organs work simultaneously I have come to understand what causes biological systems to fail and realise that, through chemical knowledge and increasing drug development, we are able to prevent these failures. Pharmacology will enable me to learn about drugs and their applications, the ways in which they are essential in prolonging life, and make a career as a research pharmacologist both rewarding and stimulating.

Within biology I have studied antibiotics and have been particularly fascinated with the topic of resistance. Understanding how mutations within the DNA sequences of bacteria lead to resistance of antibiotics was interesting, yet alarming due to the level of resistance there will be in the near future. My time at a community pharmacy really underlined the degree to which antibiotics are used within medicine and the reliance we have upon them. By witnessing the way the pharmacist advised customers, I became aware of the demand upon pharmaceutical companies to develop new antibiotics and am keen to be part of this. Studying A level Chemistry has allowed me to work upon my practical skills, allowing me to think methodically and evaluate results and draw conclusions. Experimental work on the synthesis of aspirin again highlighted the key link between chemistry and pharmacy. Through molar and pH calculations, in combination with studying mathematics, I have been able to develop my problem-solving abilities, which I feel will aid my learning at university.

My work experience reinforced my underlying interest in pharmacology. Having spent two weeks at a local community pharmacy I saw how the role of a pharmacist has developed beyond prescribing, to the provision of valuable health checks, including blood and cholesterol checks and diabetes screening, and also the advice and follow-on support needed for long-term medication. I was fortunate to spend time in a laboratory at my local university, seeing how experiments over a long period of time are needed to understand the side-effects of drugs and how a breakthrough, such as the recent one for treatment of Alzheimer's, will come after years of painstaking research.

I look forward to the prospect of studying a challenging course that will lead me into the ever-developing field of pharmacology. I will continue to be conscientious, inquisitive and open minded as I enter the next stage of my academic life.

Personal skills and qualities

A personal statement should not only demonstrate your passion for the subject but should show who you are as a person and therefore show you as a potential asset to university life. This section is very important but shouldn't take up any more than a third of the total statement, as the main focus should be on the subject.

First draft

In the summer of 2016, I helped set up a medical camp for a socially deprived village in the Punjab, India which focused on diseases of the eye. I initially helped in the fundraising side of the project by organising events such as car boot sales and sports events, raising £1,200. On the trip, I talked to patients, carrying out duties such as cleaning and serving food.

Through my school career, I was elected senior prefect by my fellow students and organised events, taking forward student issues. I am a keen cricketer, playing for my local cricket club. In addition to playing league matches, I also help out with coaching the junior members. I have achieved my Duke of Edinburgh's Bronze Award and also an ECKA-approved black belt in karate. The latter was a goal that took me six years to achieve.

Comments

This draft tells the admissions tutor that the student has undertaken a range of activities and responsibilities and it would be possible to deduce the skills and qualities gained from them. However, the student needs to be much more reflective, moving beyond a list of what s/he has done and exploring what is demonstrated about their character, linking implicitly or explicitly (where relevant) to what is required for their pharmacology degree.

Final version

In the summer of 2016 I witnessed care in a very different environment where I helped set up a medical camp for a socially deprived village in the Punjab, India which focused on diseases of the eye. Patients were screened by local doctors and any diseases were treated with medicines and, where required, surgery for cataracts was performed. The importance of the antibiotics and drugs specific to these diseases was evident to me and I became aware of just how much we took for granted in the UK. On the trip, I spent time talking to patients, carrying out duties such as cleaning and serving food, building my communication and empathy skills. These interpersonal qualities are essential for working in a research team and communicating findings to pharmaceutical companies.

Through my school career, I have demonstrated important skills of commitment and responsibility, being elected senior prefect by my fellow students and organising events and taking forward student issues. I see it as important to maintain my own physical fitness and I am a keen cricketer, playing for my local cricket club. In addition to playing league matches, I also help out with coaching the junior members, which has helped to develop my own leadership and team skills. I have achieved my Duke of Edinburgh's Bronze Award and also an ECKA-approved black belt in karate. The latter was a goal that took me six years to achieve and required a high level of discipline and commitment. I believe I will bring these qualities to a career as a research pharmacologist, important in a field where dedication and willingness to persevere are crucial.

Personal statement for pharmacy

If you wish to apply for pharmacy, you will need to demonstrate not only your scientific interest in chemistry and the biology of the human body, but that you are able to empathise with people and care about their health. You will need to show that you are a good communicator and someone who is active in your community. Pharmacy is more of a vocation and therefore a personal statement for this degree will have more in common with ones for medicine and dentistry.

Alisha Hussain: Year 1 MPharm student at Birmingham University

Alisha's tips for writing a personal statement:

'I was advised by my college tutor to send my UCAS application as soon as possible as places would be taken quickly and would become more competitive. In my opinion it was vital to send my application early. This would ensure that I applied to the universities most likely to be positive regarding my situation. Through making direct contact with them to discuss my circumstances, I decided on which universities I would like to apply to. I would advise any students to contact admissions tutors at the schools of pharmacy about any extenuating circumstances or unusual educational profiles as soon as possible and get any responses in writing.

'In writing their statement, I would advise students to simply begin to write, but not to start with the first paragraph or the last as these are the most difficult (although I did have an attempt in my first draft!). Students should not be scared to show their first draft to someone at their school or college as tutors are happy to advise you.

'In the first draft I included my work experience opportunities, A level subjects and some of my extra reading. Extra reading included issues such as the impact of an ageing population and antibiotic resistance. I read about nicotine replacement therapy, in particular the effectiveness of e-cigarettes and whether they should be available on the NHS. Another good topic to read about is "Should the NHS be allowed to refuse non-emergency treatment to patients unless they lose weight or stop smoking?". This could be an interesting interview question. There is some relevant information regarding the roles of pharmacists in the future available for prospective pharmacists (www.bpsa.co.uk/what-could-the-role-of-the-pharmacist-be-in-the-future) that can help a student when showing their knowledge of the profession in a personal statement.'

Alisha's first draft:

My motivation to study pharmacy comes from my desire to learn about the formation of pharmaceutical drugs as well as the social interaction with patients and other members of staff within a multi-disciplinary team. A concerning issue for today's profession is electronic delivery cigarette systems. Some believe that e-cigarettes have glamourised cigarettes with the various flavours on offer. However it may be possible that these systems are more effective than nicotine replacement therapies (NRT). According to the *Pharmaceutical Journal* '20% of smokers said they successfully quit while using e-cigarettes compared with 10.1% using over-the-counter NRT and 15.4% using will power alone'. Further studies and research are required following the long-term use of these to determine if e-cigarettes are safe alternatives to NRT. Other issues I have an interest in include the over-prescribing of antibiotics which is facing not only pharmacists but other healthcare professionals too.

A-level Chemistry has expanded my knowledge in how chemical elements interact and enhanced my analytical and evaluation skills, as shown in titration experiments. Mathematics has allowed me to develop skills in processing and interpreting data using appropriate methods such as histograms, measures of location, averages and standard deviation.

I have obtained a range of relevant experiences recently. During my placement at Boots, I was able to gain first hand relevant experience of the pharmacy profession. I worked closely with a pharmacist and a dispenser on a daily basis and took great joy in being able to learn more about the profession as well as aiding the pharmacist in dispensing medicines to patients. In addition, I was given the responsibility to help some customers, albeit on a non-advisory basis.

I undertook a placement at Walsall Manor Hospital where I was able to observe a multidisciplinary team within the hospital environment. This enhanced my understanding of the importance of each member of staff in the patient's journey. In this sensitive environment I learned the importance of patient confidentiality and clear communication with all members of staff. A pharmacist is also required to display similar skills as they have a professional and legal duty to keep patient information confidential. While assisting with the teaching at Delves School, I was able to develop skills in versatility and presenting with confidence, as I was often working with different students in different ability sets; this is key to a career in pharmacy as one would be engaging with a range of patients on a daily basis. (2,613 characters)

Comments

Alisha demonstrates the relevant work experience she has undertaken and identified what she has learned. She explains what she did and makes some relevant comments. She explains about her research into NRT in the first paragraph but it becomes more of a lecture than an opportunity to develop how she is interested in pharmacy. Alisha mentions her A level subjects, but does not say anything about her wider interests and extra-curricular activities. The statement is short at 2,613 characters when she has 4,000 available to her.

Alisha's final draft that led to her receiving offers from all five universities:

My motivation to study pharmacy comes from my desire to learn about the formation of pharmaceutical drugs as well as the social interaction with patients and other members of staff within a multidisciplinary team. I have a particular interest in the operation of hospital pharmacies. I feel I would be better suited to a hospital environment as I have the IT skills for recording information and the ability to solve problems using scientific knowledge in order to calculate dosages methodically in order to avoid mistakes.

I have obtained a range of relevant experience in pharmacies which has helped me to understand the demands of the profession. During my placement at Boots, I worked closely with a pharmacist and a dispenser on a daily basis and took great joy in being able to learn more about the profession as well as aiding the pharmacist in dispensing medicines to patients. In addition, I was given the responsibility to help some customers, albeit on a non-advisory basis. In order to ensure that patients who have memory/learning difficulties are taking the right medications cassette boxes were prepared so each day would have a specified compartment. From my work experience I was able to obtain knowledge of Medicine Use Reviews (MURs). MURs are clinical medication reviews with the pharmacist and the patient that review patients taking medicines for long-term conditions. In this consultation pharmacists will clarify any difficulties in understating in patients' medication, make motions for patients suffering from side-effects where possible and reduce medicine wastage.

I undertook a placement at Walsall Manor Hospital where I was able to observe a multidisciplinary team within the hospital environment. This enhanced my understanding of the importance of each member of staff in the patient's journey. In this sensitive environment I learned the importance of patient confidentiality and clear communication with all members of staff. A pharmacist is also required to display these skills as they have a professional and legal duty to keep patient information confidential. While assisting with the teaching at Delves School, I was able to develop skills in versatility and presenting with confidence as I was often working with different students in different ability sets; this is key to a career in pharmacy as one would be engaging with a range of patients on a daily basis.

A-level Chemistry has expanded my knowledge of how chemical elements interact and enhanced my analytical and evaluation skills, as shown in titration experiments. Mathematics has allowed me to develop skills in processing and interpreting data using appropriate methods such as histograms, measures of location, averages and standard deviation.

From my wider reading, I have become particularly interested in the debate regarding electronic cigarettes. A concerning issue for today's profession is electronic delivery cigarette systems. According to the *Pharmaceutical Journal* '20% of smokers said they successfully quit while using e-cigarettes compared with 10.1% using over-the-counter NRT and 15.4% using will power alone'. Further studies and research are required following the long term use of these to determine if e-cigarettes are safe alternatives to NRT. I believe that e-cigarettes are being marketed as much less addictive to normal cigarettes with unforeseen long-term effects, with chemicals flavourings that are not necessarily safe when inhaled.

My involvement in the debating club has enabled me to develop my skills in research, public speaking, critical thinking, teamwork and leadership. One debate I found particularly interesting was whether Britain should pay reparations in order to make amends to its former colonies.

I am looking forward to playing an active role in university life with my passion for learning pharmacy. I believe I have the relevant skill set and experience to excel in this area.

Comments

Alisha has interwoven her experiences and wider reading much more effectively to demonstrate why she is interested in pharmacy and in what ways she can demonstrate the skills necessary to succeed in this field. She gives much more information about her work experience placements and also refers to her skills in debating. Alisha is much more specific in explaining what she did during her work experience and what she learned from it, convincing any admissions tutor of her genuine interest in pharmacy.

Finally

The above statements have been amended for content rather than accuracy. With a limited number of lines and characters available, you need to be clear and concise, ensuring that spelling and punctuation are correct as well as organising your ideas effectively. I have known students who are fully capable of undertaking a degree course in pharmacy or pharmacology rejected because of the poor quality of their statement: carelessness indicates to the admissions tutor that you do not have the commitment or attention to detail needed for both these degrees.

7 | Interviews

You have submitted your UCAS application and, while you are waiting for the universities' decisions, some universities will invite you for an interview. Fundamentally, the interview is designed for the university to find out whether you are genuinely interested in the course, have the skills and relevant knowledge needed to cope with the content and will fit well into the department. Above all, it is looking for potential and for someone who is willing to learn.

For many of you, this will be the first time you have had an interview. Even if you have a part-time job, you may not have had a formal interview, or you had one over the telephone. As you prepare for the interview, remember that the very fact you have been invited means that your application has interested the admissions tutors and this is an opportunity to confirm the impression you have given them and for them to find out more about you and the information provided in your personal statement.

As I discussed in Chapter 6, it is important that your personal statement is an accurate reflection of you and the experiences, research and skills that you possess. I have known students get themselves in dreadful messes in interviews because they have been economical with the truth – claiming to have read books they have only glanced at, to have been regular readers of journals read once or having made a work experience placement out to be longer or more productive than it was. Interviewers want to meet the real you, not what you think they want in a prospective student.

Check the email account you have entered on your UCAS form, as some universities will send interview details directly to you via email rather than by post. Students have been rejected because they did not reply to offers of interview and only realised that this was the case when they saw it on their Track update.

Preparing for an interview

Practising for an interview is crucial to your success. Your school or college should have staff who can offer you practice interviews, so approach your tutor, head of year or teacher in one of your science A level subjects to ask for their help. They should have experience in interviewing students or will be able to recommend someone who can help. Friends and family can also be recruited to help you – the more you practise, the better. Practising answering questions in a clear and coherent way is definitely something that needs to be done over and over again, however confident you normally are in your communication.

It might be worth checking with the university as to how the interview will be structured so that you can practise accordingly. Some may interview with a panel, others with one or two interviewers and some may set up a group activity with several applicants to see how you work in a team and communicate with the others.

Read through your personal statement and all the information you have put on your form and write a list of the questions you feel someone would ask in order to find out more. These could include the following.

* Tell me more about the time when you …
* What do you feel you learned from your experience at …?
* What was the most challenging/rewarding part of your experience at …?
* In what ways did your experience at … confirm your interest in this course?
* Was there anything about your experience at … which surprised/confused/inspired you?
* Which of your experiences was the most rewarding/disappointing?
* You say in your statement that your experience at …. taught you … Tell me about a specific example which would show this.
* Tell me more about the way your academic project/extended project/reading of … has developed your interest in this course.

Reading in the media about the latest issues related to pharmacy and pharmacology will also improve your performance at interview. Look out for the latest developments in research; for example, breakthroughs in drugs for blood pressure were current in March 2017 and initial findings for the drug canakinumab in August 2017 showed positive outcomes in trials for reducing inflammation in the body and therefore repeat heart attacks, angina and deaths from cancer. The postcode lottery for prescribing of certain drugs is an ongoing issue, as are health campaigns which pharmacists may be supporting as an extension to the current health checks and advice for stopping smoking and combating obesity. The journal of the British Pharmaceutical Students' Association (BPSA), *Future Pharmacist*, is available to download (www.bpsa.co.uk) and, although it is intended for undergraduates, it covers current issues in pharmacy, articles relating to research projects being undertaken by students and advice on developing careers. Recent campaigns have highlighted the marketing of brand-name tablets and the lack of public awareness that they contain the same quantity of pain relief as supermarket own brands, but at up to six times the price.

Remember that pharmacy is a scientific degree, needing chemistry and – for most universities – biology, together with a reasonable level of mathematics, so do ensure that you have read through your AS and A level notes in order to be confident that you can do straightforward calculations accurately, in case you are asked as part of your interview assessment.

Finally, make sure that you have carried out up-to-date research on the university course so that you do not ask questions to which you should already know the answers! Find out information about the lecturers and professors in the relevant departments and their research interests and careers to date, including any texts or articles they have written.

Practical preparations for the interview

It is important to make sure you are on time for the interview, so make your travel arrangements as soon as possible. Check the route in advance so that you are confident about the journey and aim to be there half an hour before your interview, allowing time for traffic delays if travelling by car, and train/bus/plane delays if taking public transport. Check that you know exactly where to go once you reach the university and the availability of parking on campus. If you are in any doubt, ring for advice.

Dress smartly for the interview, with a suit or smart trousers/skirt/ dress and jacket, but make sure you are comfortable. Excessive jewellery, scarves and high heels can be distracting in the interview while facial piercings or tattoos on display can be off-putting, especially if you are applying for a course such as pharmacy or pharmacology where you are likely to have a career in the public eye.

Take with you a copy of your application, including the personal statement, and notes you have made in preparation for the interview as well as the letter of invitation and any information sent to you.

At the interview

On arrival at the university, be courteous with everyone you meet; you never know who will be invited to give feedback about you. It has been known that the seemingly random tutor who shows you to a waiting room or gives a tour turns out to be the professor who is conducting the interview. Assume you are on show for the entire time you are at the university and make sure you are professional at all times.

Your body language will make a strong impact on your interviewer; adopting an upright posture and avoiding slouching, making easy eye contact when responding to questions and not fidgeting will all contribute to a good first impression. On entering the room, offer to shake hands and greet the interviewer(s) with a polite 'Good morning' or 'Good afternoon', using their name(s) if you know them. Wait to be asked to sit down and then give yourself a moment to be settled and comfortable. When you are asked a question, take time to think about your answer rather than diving into it in an unstructured way and don't be afraid to ask for clarification if you are uncertain as to what they are asking. If there is more than one interviewer, make eye contact initially with the one who asked the question, but then include the others so that it is clear you are talking to them all. Take notice of their body language; if your answer is lengthy, check for signs of restlessness or indications that they are waiting to ask their next question, as they will have a time limit for each interview and could have a tight schedule for the day.

General questions which could be asked include the following.

* Why would you like to come to this university?
* Why do you want to study pharmacy/pharmacology?
* What is it about this course that makes it the right one for you?
* Tell me about a time when you faced a difficult challenge and how you handled it.
* What do you consider to be a strength/weakness of yours?
* What future career plans do you have/where do you see yourself in 10 years' time?
* Which subject have you particularly enjoyed at A level and why?
* What aspects of your A level study have you found to be the most demanding and why?
* What additional reading and research have you done which has taken you beyond your A level specification in one of your subjects?

More subject-specific questions will include those given above relating to the personal statement and application form. They may also focus on some of the following areas.

* How have specific areas of A level study linked to your interest in pharmacy/pharmacology?
* Which current health campaigns and scientific breakthroughs have interested you?
* What does MRSA stand for?
* Name three ways we isolate/discover drugs.
* Name a prescription-only-medicine (POM) and what it does.
* Why does insulin have to be administered intravenously only?
* What is antibacterial resistance? How does it occur?
* What can one do to prevent resistance?
* Name three ways a pharmacist helps to promote health in the community.
* Name some drugs which you will find exclusively in a hospital pharmacy.

- Questions based on relevant ethical issues related to the course/ career may also feature, for example dispensing of the contraceptive pill to under-16s, drug alternatives for addicts, refusing to sell more than a certain amount of over-the-counter medication, rationing of drugs and who should be given them, funding for research and testing on animals as well as human volunteers, determining priority for treatment and whether it should be given to those considered to be responsible in some way for their own condition.

You may be given specific scenarios to test your response to an ethical dilemma which may be related to pharmacy or pharmacology directly or to an issue which could relate to the interviewer's personal experience. For example, some ethical scenarios to practise might include the following.

- You are in a supermarket with a friend and s/he tells you that s/he is going to steal something and it is not the first time. What do you do?
- A friend or relative tells you that they regularly buy an over-the-counter drug, such as Nytol, to help them sleep, and take more than the prescribed dose. What do you do?
- You are working in a pharmacy or in a supermarket and someone without ID asks to buy a product with an age restriction, such as medication, alcohol or cigarettes. After you refuse, they return with a 'friend' who happens to have ID, but you suspect that it is fake and/or the purchase is for the original customer. What do you do?
- You are concerned about a friend/relative who has lost a significant amount of weight and you believe them to be lying about what they eat or about making themselves sick after eating. They insist they are fine; what do you do?
- A friend/relative tells you that they are able to buy, over the internet, prescription drugs, such as those intended for ADHD, because they have heard they will increase their concentration and allow them to study longer. What do you do?

> In your answers try to build in reference, where relevant, to your own experience, reading and research on the university course.

At the end of the interview, you may be given the opportunity to ask questions. You do not have to do so and it is better to say no than to ask something to which you should know the answer. You could consider asking the following questions.

- What further experience or reading should I undertake to prepare me for this course?
- I was interested in your question about … Can you tell me what you think about this?

* I have been interested in your research into … Can you tell me what inspired you to undertake it?
* I'm interested in … as a career route. Have any of your graduates gone into this area?
* How did you get to the role you are in today?
* What advice would you give someone of my age who wishes to be a pharmacist/researcher/clinical pharmacologist?
* If they have not mentioned it, you could ask when and how you will hear about the outcome of the interview and whether they make offers which are different from the standard one published on their website.

Pharmacology interview: University of Manchester

About 4,500 students apply for biomedical and biological courses at the University of Manchester each year and 650 are offered places. Manchester interviews all students applying for these courses, and this includes their BSc Pharmacology undergraduate course.

Applicants are selected for interview based on their predicted grades, reference and the personal statement. Questions at interview are based on the personal statement, so if the prospective student is also applying for medicine, dentistry, veterinary science or pharmacy at Manchester or elsewhere, the department realises that the personal statement will focus on this other course. In this situation, if invited for interview, students are asked to send an additional personal statement by email to arrive no later than the Friday before the interview to allow the interviewer time to read it. The applicant should be prepared to answer questions based on topics they have mentioned in their personal statement as well as:

* why pharmacology?
* why Manchester?
* questions on their interests and experiences related to pharmacology, such as wider reading and work experience
* questions on their non-academic interests and activities.

The interview is also an opportunity for prospective undergraduate students to find out more about the department, for example whether the pharmacology degree and style of teaching will suit them. They are encouraged to ask questions at the interview so they can make an informed choice. Even if applicants have already attended an Open Day, they are asked to come for the full interview day, including an introductory talk, tour of the department with student ambassadors and a practical demonstration in the laboratory.

Reproduced with kind permission from the University of Manchester.

Once the interview is definitely concluded, remember to thank them for their time and say that you have enjoyed meeting them and visiting the university again. Ensure you are equally polite to anyone you see again on your way out.

Remember that the interview process is not just an opportunity for the department to find out about you, but for you to discover more about whether this is the right university and course for you. You will be spending the next three to five years at the university and in this department, if you are lucky enough to be offered a place, so it is important that you still feel you would want to choose it as either your firm or insurance choice.

'Applicants are invited to interview with a member of academic staff and a current student. We are looking for enthusiasm and commitment to pharmacy and that the student has done some research on not just pharmacy and the role of a pharmacist but also studying pharmacy at Bradford. We ask the student to relate their current/recent studies to subjects relevant to pharmacy and ask a couple of reflective questions around their values to ensure they are congruent with those of a future healthcare professional. Because our programme is taught predominately by an active learning strategy called team-based learning (TBL), we invite the students to participate in a TBL taster to ensure they like and will benefit from this style of learning. This isn't currently assessed and there is no written assessment.

'At the interview we look for evidence of the skills they have mentioned in their application to see that they communicate effectively and that they possess values congruent with those of a future healthcare professional. These personal qualities include the ability to work with others, to reflect on their experiences and relate them to those of caring healthcare professional. We are really looking for evidence of their commitment and dedication to study pharmacy with an understanding of current pharmacy practice, so we might ask them for examples of what a pharmacist does from day to day and their role in preventing illness. We have approximately four to five applications each year for each available place on our MPharm degree.'

Simon Tweddell: Director of Admissions at University of Bradford

Interview with Lee Buttery: Admissions Tutor at University of Nottingham

How do you judge a UCAS application in order to decide whether to interview/offer a place?

'Naturally, due to the competitive nature of our course we are looking for students who have excellent academic achievement, but we're also looking for applicants who show a genuine enthusiasm and interest in the course and in working in the industry. That said, we do also look at candidates with interests in healthcare and who might be applying for other courses as a first choice, like medicine.'

What are the specific features of your interview process?

'All candidates are interviewed, either in person within the school or via Skype, which is mainly used for international candidates. Interviews are scheduled every two to three weeks from November to March during the UCAS application cycle. The interview takes the format of a number of multi-mini interview stations, which assess communication skills, interests and general knowledge of pharmacy, ethics and professional values, basic science of how medicines work, numeracy and a group exercise to assess ability to interact with and engage with their peers. Apart from the group exercise, which lasts 30 minutes, most stations last 5 minutes and involve face-to-face discussion with members of staff. Importantly, the interview session includes a general overview of the course and the University of Nottingham, a briefing about the interview (candidates also receive details of the interview via email when they are invited to attend) and a talk by/with our current students.'

What qualities and skills are you judging in an interview?

'Good communication skills, enthusiasm for and interest in pharmacy and healthcare, strong professional values and empathy, and an ability to work with others. Experience of pharmacy is not essential or required. The interview is also an opportunity for the candidate to assess if pharmacy and Nottingham are right for them!'

Do you accept retake students?

'We do accept candidates who retake exams and the entry requirements are the same as for all applicants – i.e. higher grades are not requested.'

What scholarships and bursaries do you offer?

'Around a third of our undergraduate students are likely to be eligible for our core bursary, which offers up to £2,000 for each year of undergraduate study.'

What areas of pharmacy do your students go into for their pre-registration training and careers?

'The majority of our graduates go into community practice, with smaller numbers going into hospital and fewest of all going into industry. Importantly, just about all of our graduates are in employment after graduating and completing their pre-registration training. A number of graduates return to higher education after qualifying to complete PhDs.'

Case study: Isobel Sharma, Year 1 pharmacy student at the University of Nottingham

'To be honest, I initially decided to do pharmacy because I was told by my previous school that I wouldn't get the grades required to do dentistry. In Year 9/10 I began to investigate pharmacy and when I had to do work experience in Year 11 I decided to apply to local community pharmacies. I feel that I was lucky to get three placements, all of which I really enjoyed and which made me realise pharmacy was the right choice for me. My placements were at two Lloyds pharmacies, in completely different socioeconomic areas, and at one private community pharmacy. In each of the different pharmacies I saw different services provided that were relevant to the location of the pharmacy. For example, at the lower socioeconomic pharmacy, drug abuse programmes were offered, whereas the private community pharmacy offered things such as pre-prepared medicine trays and services to the elderly. I've always been interested in why and how things work, even as a child I was very nosy according to my parents, so pharmacy seemed like the perfect fit as I would be studying how different drugs affect the body and how they help/make people feel better

'Because I retook a year of my A levels, I applied for pharmacy twice. The first time I applied to Aston, Reading, Brighton, Portsmouth and De Montfort and the second time to Birmingham, Aston, Nottingham, Keele and Liverpool John Moores. Birmingham and Portsmouth both gave me offers without interview. I can remember some details about the interviews, for example that basic maths tests were given, either on the day or online in advance and that at Brighton and Liverpool John Moores we had to take part in a group interview and show your teamwork skills. De Montfort provided us with mock interview materials and as part of the interview there were scenarios to read and assess, focusing on ethical situations. Keele had a one-to-one interview with generic questions about my interest in pharmacy and a focus on my personal statement.

'I was very lucky to get into the University of Nottingham thanks to the preparation I had done with my college; it was the hardest interview I have quite frankly ever done! I think it was because no-one seemed to know what to expect. There was a group exercise with an ethical scenario to explore. We had a five-minute maths test, in which you had to do nine questions without a calculator, and this was a mixture of conversions, decimals, fractions and long division. There was also a five-minute "science" test that contained biology and chemistry questions. There was a question about drugs and their role in my test. After we did the tests and the group exercises, the last part of the interview was the MMI stations (multiple mini interview). There were four or five stations and you had a minute to read over a sheet of paper that had the questions that the interviewers would ask you, so you could prepare in a way. Each of these stations lasted four minutes. From what I remember there was one about chemistry so I had to say what an acid was (H+ donor) and balance an equation of HCL + MgNaOH. There was an ethics station with situations based on the pharmacy ethics information available on the University of Nottingham website. There was also another station where I was asked why I wanted to study pharmacy and the difference between types of pharmacies. It was very intense to say the least. I didn't think I would get an offer because I felt that the interview had gone so badly, yet the day after I received an email stating they were giving me an offer! I think this goes to show that you can never really judge for yourself how an interview has gone.

'A useful piece of advice to applicants would be to google the universities as much as possible and try to find out any information about the interviews or the course itself, so you can ask a relevant question. Universities like students who ask them questions.

'What helped me get offers was firstly my solid personal statement that gave me the opportunity to attend interview. The personal statement is like the base of a tree for example, the roots that hold the tree down and stabilise it, with each aspect of my experience being a separate branch. In addition to my academic study, I did many extracurricular activities, including my bronze and silver Duke of Edinburgh (DofE). For the physical aspect of my DofE I played golf, for the skills aspect I did guitar and cooking, and for the volunteering parts I worked at a charity shop and volunteered at a special needs school for two years. I think volunteering at the special needs school helped my application stand out. Firstly,

I gained communication skills. Not all of the children could speak or were able to understand so I picked up some basic sign language. I also adjusted myself to the children I was working with, by changing my attitude so they would feel comfortable with me. I think volunteering to help people is a good way to set your application apart from the rest. This could be by volunteering at a care home or a school for example.

'I also think having work experience helps. Although the universities understand it is hard for everyone to get work experience, I would recommend trying to get some even if it is only a few days. I would also say try to get work experience at a hospital, or somewhere other than a community pharmacy. I struggled with getting it because I either applied too late or was too young, so I'd say apply early but ensure you are at least 16–18 years old.

'I also think being honest helped me get offers. I admit that things didn't go right for me the first time I sat my A levels so I went back and did them again. When I was asked why I didn't do as well as I hoped, I admitted that I lacked the right exam technique, but I was developing it in my retake year.'

My experiences so far and what I think about the university I am attending:

'I am currently attending the University of Nottingham, MPharm four-year course and I am in Year 1.

'So far I am enjoying it, but it can be tiring after the large period of time I had off in the summer. There are many contact hours on this course, at least 20 a week – nine to five with only an hour-long lunch break is becoming a regular occurrence! However, I knew that pharmacy had a lot of contact hours before I applied, so it is just a matter of getting used to it. The university has a system called "Moodle" which is very good. The lecturers record their lectures and put up podcasts, so you can go back and revisit any lecture you would like. They also put up extra materials such as supplementary slides and questions which are also useful. Because I have only been studying here for five weeks, I feel like I can't answer this question as fully as I would like!'

Ideas about what I would like to do in the future:

'In the future I would love to go into cosmetics. Researching and producing new products that are needed in the industry. I would also like to work in a hospital. I think by having a pharmacy degree you can go into anything you want, whether it be community pharmacy, industry, hospital, you name it!'

Case study: Daniela Gennuso, Year 1 pharmacy student at the University of Nottingham

'I studied biology, chemistry and history A level and chose pharmacy as a degree (and eventual profession) partially based on my interest in science in school and how the subject applied the areas of biology (human biology and cellular biology) and chemistry (primarily organic and also physical) in a clinical setting. I have always been the type of person who likes to have a plan, so it appealed to me that pharmacy offered a clear profession to enter but also gave so many options as to the area of pharmacy that I could work in.

'My work experience in a local community pharmacy gave me a good insight into just how patient-focused pharmacy is as a degree and profession and the way in which the science you learn is applied in practice. During my work experience, I asked the pharmacist plenty of questions about what services they provide and what they thought were important qualities for a pharmacist to possess, finding this to be the most common interview question I received.

'For personal statements I think it was important to make a link between each point you made about yourself and how this demonstrates your interest in pharmacy as a career (scientific or patient-related) or demonstrated a skill such as communicating effectively and how this will be valuable experience for your degree. Furthermore, it is also important to demonstrate a clear knowledge of what pharmacists do throughout your personal statement.

'The majority of the interviews I attended (Cardiff, Hertfordshire, Bath, Reading) had a very relaxed interview style, asking generic questions such as: "Why pharmacy? Why this university?", "What qualities should a pharmacist have?" and questions about your current subjects and what you find the most interesting. Some also asked if I knew of any pharmacy-related news, and Cardiff University had a short maths test covering basic arithmetic. The University of Nottingham employed a MMI-style interview with six stations — communication, ethical, or science-based — at which you completed in short mini interviews, plus a non-calculator maths test and a short science test. My best advice for the interviews is to be as relaxed and natural as possible as the majority of the universities just want to check you aren't socially inept!

'I am currently in my first year and am really enjoying the course so far. The course here is really well- integrated, so all the science taught blends really well with the patient care; everything relates directly to becoming a pharmacist. It is early days, but I am hoping to graduate, complete my pre-registration year in a hospital and eventually become a hospital pharmacist.'

8 | Non-standard applications

So far we have looked at what may be considered to be the 'standard' university application from UK students who have studied A levels in the relevant science subjects – chemistry with some combination of biology and mathematics or physics. But what happens if you did not take science at A level, or you are from overseas, a mature student or even a graduate? What happens if you wish to study pharmacy or pharmacology outside the UK or have a disability or special educational needs? This chapter will look at the implications for you and how to go about making a successful application.

Those who have not studied science A levels

If you have decided that you wish to study for a degree in pharmacy or pharmacology, having already started a programme of A levels (or their equivalent – Scottish Highers, IB, etc.) which does not include any of the necessary science subjects, there are different routes open to you.

You do need to have the equivalent of the A level knowledge in order to be accepted onto a degree course, and either this can be gained through taking a further two years at a sixth-form college (effectively taking the relevant science A levels from scratch) or there is the option of an intensive one-year course. For the latter, you would need to research colleges carefully, as they are likely to consider your suitability for such an intensive course on an individual basis – taking account of your scientific background at GCSE, performance in your other A level subjects and aptitude for science.

For both pharmacy and pharmacology courses, universities offer degrees with a Foundation year. This is an additional year to the usual three- or four-year degree, taken in your first year of university, and is used for students who do not have A level knowledge of science. For example, the University of East Anglia states in its summary on the UCAS course search that 'The Foundation Year course gives you the chance to study on our prestigious MPharm degree if you don't meet the traditional entry criteria. You may be a mature student looking for a new career, someone who missed out on studying A levels or a student without a science background who wishes to change direction.

Whatever the case, we'll assess your individual circumstances and, if successful, you'll be given a thorough introduction to the basics of biology, chemistry and mathematics and key pharmacy.'

Universities will be looking for candidates who have the potential, commitment and aptitude to succeed in scientific areas and are willing to develop their skills. To apply for a degree with a Foundation year, students must therefore be able to demonstrate, through either additional reading or extensive work experience, that they are committed to the subject for which they are applying.

Case study: Matthew Stibbs, a successful Foundation year student

Matthew Stibbs, now an admissions tutor at a pharmacy school, is an excellent example of a student who took the Foundation year route into an MPharm degree.

'I took my GCSEs and then completed A levels by distance learning in business, economics and law while working part time as a pharmacy technician at Lloyds Pharmacy. My A levels were not in the appropriate science qualifying subjects so I took the Health Foundation year at Keele University and found the approach very supportive, with teaching followed up by problem-solving sessions. I achieved the required 70% in the end of year examinations and was accepted onto the MPharm degree. After graduating, I completed my pre-registration year at the same branch of Lloyds Pharmacy where I continued to work throughout my degree, and passed the examination to register with the GPhC. I became Pharmacy Manager at Lloyds and worked there for four years, finding my A levels in business and economics useful since being a manager involves running a business. I returned to Keele as an admissions tutor and teach in the School of Pharmacy. At the same time, I continue to work part-time as a locum at Lloyds. My own experience of the Health Foundation course and of working in a community pharmacy has supported me in my admissions role at Keele.'

Overseas students

The numbers of overseas students accepted onto pharmacy courses tend to be low. Many overseas students are likely to be applying with qualifications that are not equivalent to A levels or other acceptable qualifications such as the International Baccalaureate (IB) or the Irish Leaving Certificate. If this is your situation, you need to realise that the universities will require you to have an educational background recognised as being equivalent to A levels. The pharmacy school and pharmacology department websites will usually state their entrance requirements in terms of A levels, IB, Scottish Highers, the Irish Leaving Certificate and other equivalent qualifications but, if you are studying for other qualifications, it is best to contact university admissions offices directly to ask their advice. The UCAS website also has a link to the UK government's education qualifications website, where you can check whether your examinations are suitable.

If you do not have the requisite qualifications, and this is particularly important in chemistry and at least one other science, usually biology, you will need to think about following a one-year A level programme (studying biology, chemistry and another subject). In order to manage the linguistic demands of the course, you will also need to demonstrate proficiency in English and, in most cases, will be asked to have an IELTS (International English Language Testing System) score of at least 7.0 for pharmacy. For pharmacology, this level may be slightly lower at 6.5.

Advice from the Pharmacy Schools Council

The Pharmacy Schools Council advises that international students must realise that the degree is not the end of the process of qualifying as a pharmacist, and this can have additional implications for overseas students. As has been outlined in previous chapters, after the successful completion of the course you will receive an MPharm degree. There are a number of further steps to go through before you will be able to register with the GPhC and practise as a qualified pharmacist in the UK. Once you have completed an MPharm you will need to apply for a pre-registration year. This is where you will further develop the skills you gained during your degree, as a paid employee in a professional environment. Entrance into a pre-registration year is competitive and there is no guarantee that you will receive a place. A proportion of these pre-registration places are with the NHS, but the majority of placements involve working with community pharmacists. International students are also very likely to require a visa, which can be dependent on meeting a number of conditions, including a minimum salary requirement. Prospective students should contact the United Kingdom Border Agency (www.gov.uk/browse/visas-immigration/student-visas).

Other challenges for overseas students lie in the application process itself. Students from the UK can be at an advantage, since they will have staff at their schools and colleges who can provide advice on making a successful application, particularly with regard to the personal statement and the reference. Students who are unfamiliar with UCAS applications often write unsuitable personal statements which concentrate too much on non-essential information (prizes, awards, responsibilities) and not enough on matters relevant to pharmacy and pharmacology. Admissions tutors will be interested to know why you wish to study in the UK rather than in your home country, and your experience of education at A level or equivalent in the UK, where relevant, can be helpful. Detailed advice on the personal statement can be found in Chapter 6 of this book. The person providing your reference needs to understand what pharmacy schools and departments of pharmacology are looking for in the reference. The UCAS website is a valuable source of information and guidance for referees (www.ucas. com/advisers/references).

Interviews

Many universities will require prospective students to be interviewed, especially for pharmacy, and so it is worth contacting them to see whether you would need to travel to the UK, and to make any arrangements well in advance.

Mature students and graduates

Mature students who have the required A levels but who have either taken another first degree or gone into work immediately after completing their sixth form study are of interest to universities for both pharmacy and pharmacology, as they bring life experience, maturity and a commitment to their studies.

Mature students without the relevant A levels can take the routes outlined above. There are also Access to Higher Education courses in sciences which prepare students over the age of 19 for science degrees if they do not have the necessary A levels or equivalent, for example the Access to HE Diploma in Pharmaceutical and Biomedical Science or in Science run by the City of Westminster College, which are full-time, one-year courses suitable for adults. Stanmore College has a one-year Access to HE Pharmacy and Biomedical Science course which can also enable students to progress to degree level. It is important to check the requirements of the universities to which you wish to apply for both pharmacy and pharmacology to see if they would accept the Access course you are planning to take and the levels they require you to achieve, preferably before embarking on it.

In your UCAS application, it is important to bear in mind what the admissions tutor will be looking for in relation to you being a mature student or graduate and what you can bring to university life and the course itself. These aspects should be identified in the personal statement in addition to the areas already outlined in Chapter 6 on personal statements, with relevant work experience for pharmacy and evidence of wider reading for pharmacology

Studying outside the UK

With degree courses in the UK for pharmacy being competitive, more UK students, particularly those with relatively modest A level grades, are looking abroad for other options.

There are some pharmacy undergraduate courses close to home in Europe which are largely delivered in English, and there is now a central application service for EU universities which operates in a similar way to UCAS for the UK institutions, called Eunicas (www.eunicas.co.uk). These programmes are offered by some of Europe's leading research universities and by some excellent universities of applied sciences and university colleges, which are career-orientated institutions. There is a concentration of pharmacy courses in Eastern Europe, the duration for which is five years. See the Eunicas website for more information on courses available.

There is currently not the demand to study pharmacology overseas in the same way as pharmacy, but some university courses offer international study opportunities and are referred to in Chapter 3, Choosing your course.

The tuition fees abroad are generally lower than they are in the UK and generally the cost of living is lower too. The decision to study abroad should not be taken lightly, though, as some British students find the adjustment to life in a different country more difficult than they had anticipated. If a student qualifies as a pharmacist outside the European Economic Area then, in addition to the usual 52 weeks of pre-registration training and registration assessment, they must successfully complete the Overseas Pharmacists Assessment Programme (OSPAP), a one-year postgraduate diploma currently offered by the universities of Aston, Brighton, Hertfordshire, Kingston and Sunderland. Further details on the process of qualifying can be found on www.pharmacyregulation.org.

If a student is able to adapt, then the experience has the potential to be extremely beneficial and will help to broaden their cultural horizons. Although a considerable proportion of lessons are in English, students will be required to learn the host country's language. As the course progresses, some sessions may be in the host country's language and dealing with patients and colleagues in a work environment will also require use of this language. In any event, it's not a good idea to live in a non-English-speaking country and not learn the language.

Going to university, whether at home or abroad, isn't just about studying. By studying in another country, you will have a fantastic opportunity to experience a different culture and lifestyle. If you are independent minded, with a sense of adventure and a bit of initiative, studying abroad is a life-changing experience. Studying for your undergraduate programme abroad will ensure your CV is unique.

Students with disabilities and special educational needs

Students with disabilities and special educational needs are certainly able to apply for both pharmacy and pharmacology. Universities have an equality and diversity adviser or team who will give guidance and support to students with specific needs.

You must ensure that any specific learning difficulty or disability is disclosed in the appropriate section of your UCAS application so that the university can provide the appropriate support from the start of your course. It is also important to remember that your application will not be discriminated against based on a disability or special educational needs; your application will be considered solely on the basis of your academic skills and potential and other abilities.

You should consider, however, that pharmacy makes particular physical demands on you, in terms both of working in a community, hospital or industrial placement and of handling medicines in a safe and accurate way. As a result, any physical disability that may interfere with your ability to meet these demands may make pharmacy unsuitable as a career option. If you are unsure about how your disability will affect you in these areas, then it is worth contacting the universities so that you can be individually assessed.

Anyone applying to register as a pharmacist must demonstrate their fitness to practise. The GPhC has issued guidance to all schools of pharmacy offering accredited MPharm degrees, Foundation degrees and OSPAP (Overseas pharmacists' assessment programme) courses to provide them with advice on how to develop and apply consistent fitness-to-practise procedures for students. Guidance on this can be found on the website www.pharmacyregulation.org/education/pharmacist/student-code-conduct.

Pharmacology makes demands in terms of practical assessments and laboratory work, for which study at A level or its equivalent in science subjects will have prepared you. Again, the universities will need to make reasonable adjustment and not discriminate against you on the basis of your disability or special educational needs.

It is worth contacting the team at each university where you wish to study in advance of applying, so as to discuss the support it can offer you during your studies. Visiting and talking to the team will enable you to feel much more confident about your studies and the accommodation on offer. Students with physical or mental disabilities can often stay in a hall of residence for the full three or four years of their degree course, to give stability. Chapter 10, Fees and funding, provides more details about the Disabled Students' Allowance and ways of applying for this.

9 | Results day

Once you have made your application and sat your exams, all that's left is to eagerly await the all-important results. After two months of anticipation, results day arrives. Scottish Highers results are issued approximately two weeks earlier than A levels, with A level results on the third Thursday in August. How you approach the results and the decisions you need to make on the day and in the following week will have a major impact on your success in studying pharmacy and pharmacology. This chapter is designed to take you through these stages and enable you to make informed choices, knowing the options available to you as well as how and where to get information and support.

By the time results day comes, you are likely to fit into one of the following categories.

* You are holding a firm and, if you are lucky, an insurance offer from your original choices.
* You are holding a firm offer gained through UCAS Extra.
* You are not holding an offer but are intending to apply through Clearing or take a gap year and apply in the next cycle.

Practical preparations you should make for results day

Schools and colleges release results in different ways; some will provide students with the opportunity to access them online by means of a personal login from 6am on the morning of results day. This approach has the benefit of privacy and early access to results, with the opportunity for family members to provide support and, hopefully, celebrate achievements and the associated confirmation of a university place at either the firm or insurance choice. However, many sixth forms still give out results at the school or college, some opting for an early-morning opening, where it is possible to provide specialist support and guidance from personal tutors, heads of year and careers and senior management. These members of staff will have considerable experience in guiding students to resolve any problems associated with results and university places, helping with making phone calls and researching options available to you.

To be fully prepared for results day, you need to ensure that you have the following information:

* details of the time your school or college releases results and who will be available for support and when/where
* your personal login for the website if results are released electronically
* your UCAS ID, username and password and Track number, letters from universities confirming their offers and conditions to be met
* contact details of the universities from which you have offers, including telephone numbers for admissions, the department and Clearing
* access to the email address you provided on the UCAS form
* pen and paper, a fully charged mobile phone and – if possible – a parent, sibling or friend (who is not themselves dealing with results) to provide practical and emotional support.

What to do if you meet the terms of your offer

Congratulations! If you have met the conditions of your offer, your Track status will be updated from the conditional offer to show that you have been successful, with some universities sending out confirmation letters to arrive on results day. The letter or the updating of Track (which is available from 8am onwards on results day) can mean that you receive news of a place or rejection even before the results themselves; some students are offered places even if they have just missed the terms of their offer, so it is important to realise (although not generally a source of huge concern to those who have been successful in getting their place!) that an acceptance does not necessarily mean you have gained all the required grades.

Having your place confirmed on Track and receiving your confirmation letter means that your place at the university is secure and you will be sent further details of the enrolment process, accommodation and term dates. You may have applied for accommodation after receiving your firm offer and it will then be a matter of confirming the arrangement and the date from which it is available. Other universities will allocate accommodation only when students have been successful in gaining their place and you may have to apply for it post results.

If you have exceeded the terms of your offer, you will automatically be eligible for Adjustment which enables you to hold on to your existing offer up to 31 August while applying for places on courses with higher standard entry requirements.

What to do if you do not meet the grades for your firm offer

If you have missed the grades for your firm offer, but have gained the ones needed for your insurance place, the process is the same as shown above. However, it may be that your firm choice will still be willing to confirm your offer and either Track or a letter from the university concerned will clarify this for you. If the Track status for that university is still showing as CONDITIONAL it indicates that your firm choice is still in the process of making a final decision on your application and it can be beneficial to phone to indicate your commitment to it and for either you or your school/college to explain any extenuating circumstances in relation to your results, especially if they are lower than expected.

It is only once you have been officially rejected by your firm choice that your insurance choice has the opportunity to confirm your place. It will do this if you have met its offer, and students usually try to have an insurance choice which requires at least one grade lower than their firm choice. However, insurance choice universities may be prepared to be more flexible and admit you even if you have dropped one or more grades. Having said that, as pharmacy is becoming increasingly competitive and pharmacology courses are attracting high-calibre applicants, this is not in any way guaranteed. Again, a call from you or your school or college may help your case and you will have to be prepared to be patient, remembering that university departments are under huge pressure on results day and the week after.

If you have met the terms of your insurance offer, you are effectively contracted to take it and cannot apply to any other university through Clearing unless you have contacted it and been released from this offer.

What to do if you do not have a place and still wish to go to university this year

If you have not met the terms of either of your offers and the universities are not prepared to make you an offer, or if you were not holding an offer prior to results day, you need to explore the options available to you through Clearing. Students who are in this situation will automatically be allocated a Clearing number once the universities concerned have confirmed the rejection with UCAS. The allocation of the number signals that you are eligible to apply for a place through Clearing and the details of the process are available on the UCAS website, with a video and step-by-step guide. It is helpful to have read this prior to results day, even if you feel confident about your grades, so that you are prepared to deal with this eventuality.

Places available through Clearing are advertised through specific supplements in newspapers such as the *Telegraph* and each university will constantly update their course availability on their websites, which can be accessed directly or via UCAS Course Search. You can begin to check potential availability in the weeks before results, as Course Search will indicate which universities and courses still have places that have not been allocated for firm or insurance choices. From results day onwards, these will be updated regularly, taking into account the acceptance of students. The situation will change from day to day as places are confirmed to students holding offers and through Clearing, and so swift but careful action is necessary.

Making choices through Clearing is a process which requires careful thought; students are more likely to drop out of courses where they have made decisions in haste. Remember how much thought went into your original selection of course and university: you are likely to have visited it at least once and researched the courses on offer in detail and so any change in either the course or university or even both has to be given careful consideration.

The universities for which you were holding firm and insurance offers may well make you an offer for an alternative course in related areas, and again you need to avoid the temptation of immediately accepting because it fits with your original plans. While there may occasionally be opportunities to transfer to your original course once you are at the university, this cannot be assumed and is highly unlikely in the case of pharmacy, unless the university explicitly states that this may be possible. If it is, check the requirements – would you need to transfer at the end of the first year, and is it directly into the second year of your desired course or would you need to start again? Are there specific requirements in terms of your performance that you would need to meet?

Although there are time constraints, with limited places available, there is opportunity for reflection and the process is as follows.

* Find a course which is available and read the details on the university website, contacting it for further information and clarification. Checking whether a university which originally made you an offer, which you declined, is willing to consider you again is also an option as it was clearly interested in you in the first place.
* If you wish to consider a course, ring the university to see whether it will give you a verbal offer. The university will often need to ring you back and is likely to give you a timeframe in which to proceed to the next step, and will hold your offer open for this period.
* Repeat this process for as many places as you wish to consider and as are available; keep checking the UCAS website and newspapers for updates.

Some universities may ask you to send them a new personal statement or visit them for a formal or informal interview, but this is relatively rare. It is more likely to apply to students who originally held offers for medicine and wish to be considered for pharmacy. You may ask to visit if you wish to be certain of your choice, especially if you have been made more than one verbal offer or have never visited that university before.

Once you have made your choice, enter it on UCAS using your Clearing number. You can make only one selection at a time. The university will then confirm your choice and proceed in the usual way.

Other options if you do not have a place

If you are not made an offer with which you are happy during Clearing or are keen to re-apply to any of your original choices, you will need to take a gap year and re-apply in the next UCAS round.

You may decide to upgrade your A levels, and there are a number of ways of doing this, which include attending colleges which specialise in short courses or full one-year A level courses. You may decide to retake specific modules in which your scores were low, retake a whole A level or even opt for taking a new subject in one year. Recent changes to A levels mean that there are no January examinations and so you would have to wait a year before resitting full exams or modules, making gap-year planning more challenging.

Using the year to gain more work experience, voluntary work and/or a paid job, especially where you are building up relevant knowledge and skills, will impress a university. Together with retaking your A levels to achieve the grades needed, this effective use of your gap year will show commitment and determination. Do, however, check directly with the admissions tutor that they will consider you as a retake student and clarify whether the entry requirements are the same; some universities will make higher offers if you are retaking.

Whatever you do, remember to take time to review your choice of pharmacy or pharmacology and be certain that this is the right path for you. And remember, you are still young, with many years ahead of you; once you are at university, it will not matter that you took an extra year to get there. Students who have taken a gap year and made effective use of it are often much more confident when they leave home to go to university.

Chapter 8, Non-standard applications, explores further the routes for retaking A levels and Foundation courses. There are some universities that allow students to transfer internally from a similar background course to the MPharm course, but this is not stated in the prospectus or on the website, so please check with the admissions tutor/s before applying. If you have not gained a place on a single honours pharmacology course, you may like to consider courses which have modules in pharmacology, or a pharmaceutical sciences degree. Reading the information on the university websites and contacting admissions tutors in the relevant departments is important to ensure that you are getting the course you want.

What to do if you have extenuating circumstances

An application can be made to the examination board(s) for special consideration. Your Examinations Officer at your school or college has to apply on your behalf, and must have evidence of the adverse circumstances such as illness, bereavement or other serious family circumstances. You can be told whether or not the application has been accepted but not how this has affected your results. Usually, up to 5% is added to your raw mark where you are close to the grade boundary. Where you have not been able to take a paper, new regulations for the reformed specifications mean that a grade can be calculated as long as you have completed 25% of the externally assessed units. Your school or college can also write to the universities for which you are holding an offer to ask that they take any extenuating circumstances into account when they review your results and this may mean that they are prepared to take you with a lower grade in one or more subjects. Even if your school or college did not write at the time of your examinations, if your results are disappointing, it is worth making the universities aware or mentioning it to any universities you decide to approach during Clearing.

Going into pharmacy-related employment

If you are determined to have a pharmacy-related job but feel you are unlikely to achieve the grades required or are keen to start employment sooner than would be possible with a gap year and four-year degree plus pre-registration training, you could consider becoming a pharmacy assistant or technician. To qualify as a pharmacy technician you need to be registered with the GPhC and study for an accredited qualification such as the BTEC National Diploma in Pharmaceutical Science, NVQ/SVQ Level 3 Pharmacy Services or National Certificate in Pharmaceutical Science and be working in a community or hospital pharmacy. Although the practical experience of being a pharmacy technician will prepare you well for certain aspects of the MPharm, you will still need to meet the standard entry requirements or undertake Access courses or Foundation degree routes to be accepted.

Although it can seem like the end of the world when the plans you had in place are blighted by results day, remember that you do have choices. Researching carefully and using the support offered by family, friends, school or college and the universities are all ways of ensuring that you make the right decisions at this time. A degree is a large investment in time and money, and it is important to get it right.

10 | Fees and funding

Going to university is a major commitment and to begin with some students may be put off by the cost, particularly as it is now such a major investment. However, the cost of a degree course does not need to be paid up front, and most students will be able to apply for loans to cover the tuition fees and towards the cost of living. These loans do not have to be paid back until you are earning above a certain level of income and the chapter dealing with careers shows the opportunities open to you with a degree in either pharmacy or pharmacology, which would not be the case without this investment in higher education.

The amount of student loan for which you are eligible will depend – unless you are a self-financing, mature student who is independent – on parental income. Where family income is low, there are also grants available which do not need to be paid back. A pharmacy degree which takes four years will clearly cost more overall than a three-year pharmacology degree, but will lend itself more directly to a career. So what factors need to be taken into account when considering the cost of your degree? These will include the following.

* **The location of your university.** Cities are generally more expensive in accommodation and living costs but they do have the benefit of everything being on your doorstep. You need to determine what type of student lifestyle you want and can afford.
* **Living away from or at home.** Although you will receive a reduced loan, the financial benefits of living at home and not paying for accommodation are obvious, but you will need to consider if this is the right choice for you.
* **Travel.** How far are you willing to travel, in terms of regular trips either to and from your family home or from university accommodation (usually moving off campus in your second and third year) to your lectures, practicals and tutorials?
* **Where you are from.** Students from Scotland and Wales pay different fees and the costs for international students are higher than those for EU or UK students.
* **Parental finance.** Consider whether your parents are willing to support you financially.
* **Employment.** Whether or not you take on a part-time job has implications. It can impact on your studies but can also be rewarding and reduce the level of debt you will face at the end of your course.
* **Scholarships and bursaries.** Universities will usually contact you about any bursaries and scholarships to which you are entitled,

especially those which are means tested. Agreeing to have your student loan application information shared with the university will mean that it can check your eligibility and contact you directly. It is therefore worth ticking the 'yes' boxes on the UCAS form in relation to finance so that you do not lose out.

Sponsorships and scholarships

There are limited schemes directly related to pharmacy and pharmacology that provide support to students taking degrees in these areas and those schemes available may change yearly. It is important to check the websites of the universities to see what they currently have available. The information in this section is designed to give examples of the types of awards available and is not intended to be exhaustive.

Some universities, such as University College London, have undergraduate bursary schemes to support students from low income families, and they are available to students who are taking any degree subject. Students are eligible based on parental income; they are automatically assessed to see if they qualify via Student Finance. The student must indicate on their UCAS form that they will be applying for finance and are happy to share their details with Student Finance England or their applicable regional funding authority. There is no separate application form. In addition, at UCL, there is a range of scholarships that have different criteria, many of which are open to all degree subjects and UCL does not offer a scholarship specifically for pharmacy or pharmacology.

Other schemes more directly related to pharmacy and pharmacology include:

University of Bath: Faculty of Science – Pharmacy Centenary Scholarship open to British pharmacy or pharmacology students with grades AAB+ and household income of £42,620 or less.

University of East Anglia: Ivy Rose Hood Foundation Year scholarship of £3,000 towards tuition fees open to students from Norfolk and Suffolk who are taking a Foundation year in any discipline. Preference is given to mature students. The Panasonic Scholarship in the Faculty of Science is also open to pharmacy students and currently gives £1,500 per year for either tuition or maintenance.

Robert Gordon Universty: Financial award of £2,000 open to all STEM (Science, Technology, Engineering and Maths), including pharmacy, undergraduates.

Students who are interested in these awards must check the website of the relevant universities for up-to-date information about the funding given and application procedure.

International Students

Universities recognise the financial challenge that studying in the UK makes on international students and many offer scholarships. The following are examples of these and students should check the websites of universities to which they are interested in applying.

University of Brighton: International Huxley Scholarship (currently £2,000) for MSc Pharmacology and MSc Clinical Pharmacy as well as MRes Pharmaceutical and Biomedical Sciences for self-funding international students.

University of East Anglia: Pharmacy International Excellence Scholarship for self-funding international students, offering 25–50% of the tuition fees.

Prospective international students should also check the British Council website for further details of support (www.britishcouncil.org).

Hardship grants related to pharmacy

https://pharmacistsupport.org: offers grants to families of pharmacists, pre-registration trainees and pharmacy students for help with unexpected hardship in the course of their degree.

www.leverhulme-trade.org.uk: the Leverhulme Trade Charities Trust provides grants to undergraduate students who are the children, spouses, widows or widowers of pharmacists who are – or were – registered with the GPhC.

www.opencharities.org/charities/1022715: the Harold and Marjorie Moss Charitable Trust providing grants to undergraduate pharmacy students in financial need doing a first degree in pharmacy. Applications are submitted via the student's school of pharmacy, which nominates candidates for an award.

Prizes

In the course of your study in pharmacy and pharmacology, the university may offer prizes for academic excellence that carry a financial reward. At the University of East Anglia, for example, the following awards are made to MPharm students:

- Pharmacy Practice Prize (£50) for outstanding performance in the Professional Pharmacy modules and open to Year 2 students
- School of Pharmacy prize for Year 2 (£100) for the top performing student, and the Rosemont Prize for Molecular Pharmacology (£250), awarded to the Year 4 student who produces the best 'Molecular Pharmacology' project
- Royal Pharmaceutical Society Prize (£200) for the best performing Year 4 student.

Fees

UK

Students who are UK nationals will pay lower fees than international students who are not from the EU. From September 2017 tuition fees rose to a maximum of £9,250, although some universities already feel this is insufficient for them to deliver high-quality degrees and they are subject to change.

The difference for students in the UK regarding the fees they pay depends on whether their permanent residence is in England, Scotland, Northern Ireland or Wales. These differences can be summed up as follows.

- English students must pay the full fees charged by a university wherever they choose to study in the UK.
- Scottish students who opt to study at a university in Scotland do not have to pay any fees, but will do so if they choose to attend a university in England, Wales or Northern Ireland.
- Students from Northern Ireland who wish to study in Northern Ireland will pay £4,160 but the full cost of up to £9,250 in England and Scotland and £9,000 in Wales.
- Welsh students must pay the full fees charged by a university wherever they choose to study in the UK, but can accees both fee loans and fee grants (see Table 3 on page 100).

Each individual university website will give the most up-to-date information regarding fees, but the majority do charge the maximum £9,250 currently allowed. In order to do so, they have to make grants and bursaries available for students from low-income families to widen participation in higher education, so it is important to research these carefully. Scholarships which depend on performance at A level (or equivalent) or during the degree course can also reduce the financial burden for you – and for your parents! In addition, universities run hardship schemes to support students who find themselves in financial difficulties.

EU students

For EU students, the cost will also vary depending on where they choose to study in the UK. This operates on a very similar basis as for students from the UK, in that fees of up to £9,250 apply if an EU student chooses to study in England. There is no fee to pay if they study in Scotland (as long as they fulfil the eligibility criteria), and they pay the same as resident students if they attend university in Northern Ireland or Wales.

Non-EU overseas students

For these students, the cost of a three- or four-year course can be extremely high – for example, at Aston University the cost is £17,550 per year for overseas students in 2018. The pre-registration year also has to be added into the equation, and this does not include the additional expenses either of flying home during the university holidays or the alternative of paying living costs in the UK, when domestic students are likely to be returning home to live with parents.

| Student's home region | Location of university or college | | | |
	England	Scotland	Wales	Northern Ireland
England →	Up to £9,250	Up to £9,250	Up to £9,000	Up to £9,250
Scotland →	Up to £9,250	No fee	Up to £9,000	Up to £9,250
Wales →	Up to £9,250	Up to £9,250	Up to £9,000	Up to £9,250
Northern Ireland →	Up to £9,250	Up to £9,250	Up to £9,000	Up to £4,160
EU →	Up to £9,250	No fee	Up to £9,000	Up to £4,160
Non-EU →	Variable	Variable	Variable	Variable

Table 2: Tuition fees by region for courses starting in 2018

Applying for financial support

The situation regarding fees and funding for students attending universities in England, Scotland, Wales and Northern Ireland has changed significantly over the past five years, and with the likely implications of the 2016 referendum vote to leave the European Union (Brexit), there is uncertainty at the time of writing regarding the impact of Brexit on students. Northern Ireland, for example, pledged in 2017 to continue to give the same access to EU students for loans and grants as their own residents if they start courses in 2018, regardless of whether they finish after the UK exit from the EU. The table below shows the tuition fees by region as of 2018.

There is considerable variation within the UK as to how these tuition fees and maintenance costs (see below) are funded. Students apply for loans for tuition fees or, in Wales, for a combination of fee loan and fee grant. Fee loans are repaid, as are any loans for maintenance, only when the student has graduated and is in employment. In 2017, the income threshold for this was £21,000, however in October 2017 the Welsh Government agreed to lift this to £25,000. Scotland does not charge its own students tuition fees but will provide loans for Scottish students studying in fee-paying countries.

In Wales, the combination of fee loans and fee grants for tuition fees is shown in the table below:

Region of study		Maximum fee charged	Fee loan	Fee grant
Wales	→	Up to £9,000	Up to £4,046	Up to £4,954
England, Scotland and Northern Ireland	→	Up to £9,250	Up to £4,296	Up to £4,954
Private institution	→	No limit	Up to £6,165	NIL

Table 3: Fee loans and fee grants for Welsh students by region

Maintenance costs

England moved away from a combination of loans (repayable) and means-tested grants (non repayable) in 2016 so that although students from low-income households can be assessed for a higher level of funding, they will need to repay the full amount. In Wales, Scotland and Northern Ireland, there is still a combination of loans and bursaries/grants available to students and Wales has proposed an even more radical funding system for 2018 (see page 102).

Scotland provides a combination of bursary and loan up to a maximum of £7,625, with students from the highest income bracket getting a loan of £4,750. The figures provided are accurate for students starting courses in 2017–2018.

The table below shows the maximum maintenance loan for living costs made in England, Wales and Northern Ireland.

		Living at home	London	Elsewhere in the UK	Outside the UK
England loan	→	£7,097	£11,002	£8,430	£9,654
Northern Ireland loan*	→	£3,750	£6,780	£4,840	£5,770
Wales loan and grant	→	£5,358	£9,697	£6,922	£8,253

Table 4: Maintenance loans by region

Other sources of support

In addition to grants and loans for fees and maintenance, students may be eligible to apply for help with the costs of childcare or having an adult dependant and with costs related to a mental or physical disability. The student funding organisations for England, Scotland, Wales and Northern Ireland have details of the application process on their websites.

Support with payment for childcare and other costs related to dependants is shown in the table below. Childcare costs are paid at 85% of the actual costs up to the maximum weekly allowance. The actual amounts awarded are dependent on the household income.

Support need	England	Scotland	Wales	Northern Ireland
Childcare: one child →	up to £159.59 per week	£1,215 per year	up to £161.50 per week	up to £148.75 per week
Childcare: two or more children →	£273.60		£274.50	£255.00
Parents living allowance →	£50–£1,617	£1,305	up to £1,551	£50–£1,538
Adult dependant →	£2,834 per year	£2,640 per year	£2,732 per year	£2,695 per year

Table 5: Childcare/dependants support by region

For Disabled Students Allowance (DSA), it is necessary for a student to have applied for fees and/or maintenance funding, and a separate assessment will be arranged at a centre in the student's home area to calculate the level of assistance required. The payments through the Disabled Students Allowance were capped for 2017–2018 as shown in the table below:

Allowance	England	Scotland	Wales	Northern Ireland
Equipment (per course) →	£5,358	£5,160	£5,332	£5,266
Non-medical helper per year →	£21,305	£20,520	£21,181	£20,938
General allowance per year →	£1,790	£1,725	£1,785	£1,759
Travel →	N/A	Reasonable	Reasonable	Reasonable

Table 6: Disabled Students Allowance by region

Proposals for 2018 in Wales

A new system for students resident in Wales is outlined for 2018 in which students will receive support through a combination of grants and loans equivalent to the National Living Wage. There will be no tuition fee grant from 2018, instead the tuition fee will be covered by a loan. Students will be eligible for a means-tested grant for their maintenance costs, up to £11,124 for study at London universities, £9,000 elsewhere and £7,650 for students living at home. The Welsh Government estimates that a third of students will be eligible for the full grant. All students will receive a grant of £1,000 regardless of household income. Students not eligible for the full means-tested grant can get a maintenance loan for an amount up to the difference between the grant award and the maximum level of support – a combination of grant and loan. After graduation, all students will receive £1,500 towards reducing the maintenance loan when they make their first loan repayment under the Welsh Government partial cancellation scheme.

11| Careers in pharmacy and pharmacology

Before you embark on your degree in pharmacy or pharmacology, it is advisable to have a good understanding of what careers will be open to you. Pharmacology, as has been explained earlier, does not qualify you to be a pharmacist, but it certainly opens more doors to you than the stereotype of a pharmacology student would suggest; your future does not have to be in a laboratory, although that can provide a very worthwhile career. There is far more variety nowadays and flexibility is the key to success. Pharmacy, on the other hand, will qualify you, after completion of the pre-registration year, to be a pharmacist, and this chapter will give you an insight into the different options within this profession.

Pharmacology

The most recent destinations figures for pharmacology, toxicology and pharmacy graduates from the Higher Education Statistics Agency (published in 2017 for the 2015/16 cycle) show that 78% of graduates are in employment, 8% are working and studying, 10% are studying, 2% are unemployed and the remaining 2% are listed as 'other'. Study beyond graduate level is usually required for employment in the field of research and development in the pharmaceutical industry and helps to get the better graduate jobs.

Jobs related to a degree in pharmacology include being a toxicologist, research or biomedical scientist, immunologist, analytical chemist and clinical research associate, employed not only by pharmaceutical companies but in the NHS, Department of Health (DH) and also the Intellectual Property Office (IPO).

Either before or during your degree course, it is advisable to get work experience to prepare you for graduation and the search for employment. You can get in touch with a lecturer at university and offer to volunteer in their laboratory, and contact organisations such as the British Pharmacological Society to request placements in research laboratories. While graduates often go on to take a PhD, it is also possible to move into a paid job – in a pharmaceutical company as a research scientist or sales representative, for example. Other options include further study in medicine, dentistry and veterinary medicine, for which your BSc in Pharmacology will be a relevant first degree.

Research pharmacology

As a research pharmacologist, there is always the excitement of a possible discovery of a breakthrough which will lead to drugs being developed which can cure or considerably reduce the effects of illness. The survival rates from cancer have increased over the past 50 years and it is estimated that 200 million lives have been saved through the discovery of penicillin. As Isaac Asimov said, 'The most exciting phrase to hear in science, the one that heralds new discoveries is not "Eureka!" but "That's funny ..."'

However, those discoveries and the development of new medicines are possible only after painstaking research into what they can do and their side-effects. They require extensive testing before they can be approved by NICE (National Institute for Health and Care Excellence) and become available for doctors to prescribe and pharmacists to dispense for patients.

The majority of pharmacology students who go into the field of research will undertake a PhD, for example in pharmacology and neuroscience. You will need to gain funding to be eligible for a post-doctoral research project, which will be on a fixed-term contract, often for three to four years. You will be employed by a company or university which has funding for research, with a grant that pays your salary and research costs. The challenging side to this option is that you must produce and publish high-quality research or you will not get the next position. Getting funding is also very competitive and, as in any areas of science or technological innovation, you will always be racing against other researchers in your field to get papers out first.

Clinical pharmacology

Most clinical pharmacologists qualify through a degree in medicine and can go on to work in hospitals with patients after they have had training in clinical pharmacology. As Chapter 1 explains, a lecturer in clinical pharmacology may well work in different roles in a typical week, including in toxicology, either seeing patients directly or giving advice to the National Poisons Information Service. Through the National Poisons Information Service, clinical pharmacologists will advise hospitals on how to treat patients who have been poisoned – whether intentionally or unintentionally. Cases can include the accidental taking of medicines by young children in spite of child-proof caps, teenagers and young adults who may be self-harming or elderly patients who have become confused about their medication, especially where they are in the early stages of dementia and this has not been diagnosed. Every year, the media has stories about people who have suffered from carbon monoxide poisoning either in the home or when camping, and about warnings not to use barbecues inside tents being ignored, or about central heating systems not serviced. You will use the skills in laboratory work, research and report writing developed during your degree, but – as with many other degrees – can also branch out into other areas not directly linked to pharmacology, such as teaching in schools and writing.

It is more difficult to give clear guidance as to the salaries which can be commanded by pharmacology graduates, especially as further study beyond degree level is normally required. PhD studentships offer tax-free stipends of around £17,000 a year. Typical salaries for students who are in the process of completing their PhD start from £25,000. Salaries at senior level or with experience range from £35,000 to £80,000 a year, with those in industry tending to be higher than those in academia, and pharmacologists with a PhD are likely to earn more than those without.

As Chapter 1 explains, a lecturer in clinical pharmacology may well work in different roles in a typical week, including in toxicology, either seeing patients directly or giving advice to the National Poisons Information Service.

Pharmacy

Graduates from a pharmacy degree who have completed their pre-registration year can work as community pharmacists, hospital pharmacists, primary care pharmacists or as industrial pharmacists. The pre-registration year training involves a 48-week placement, usually in a community or hospital pharmacy, success in the pre-registration examination which can be taken in June or September, satisfying the 'Fitness to Practise' criteria, and registration with the GPhC as a pharmacist. Graduates are allowed three attempts to pass the examination and have to succeed in all sections. The pre-registration trainee rate of pay in a hospital pharmacy is set at £21,909 (2017) but for a community pre-registration trainee, an NHS grant of £18,440 is paid to the provider, who does not have to pass it all to the trainee. For a non-EU student, the pay causes complications with acquiring a visa as the hospital pay is sufficient for a Tier 2 visa but the community pay is not. In Scotland the grant made to providers of pre-registration placements under the Pre-registration Pharmacist Scheme (PRPS) is such that all trainees (community and hospital) are paid £22,218 (2017), which meets the requirement for Tier 2 visa. The challenges the varying pay poses in terms of non-EU students completing the pre-registration year make the five-year integrated programme currently offered by Bradford, Nottingham and UEA appealing, even though fees are payable for the fifth year and the placement does not give a salary. Fees for registering with the GPhC include a £106 application fee and £250 first examination fee.

While most pre-registration placements take place in either a community or hospital setting, a smaller proportion are split between academia and community or Clinical Commissioning Group (CCG) and hospital. In 2017 Kent, Surrey and Sussex Health Education Training Boards (HEKSS) were trialling a scheme to give trainees one day a week experience in a GP surgery. There is also the possibility of splitting the pre-registration year with an industrial placement; one of the best ways to apply for these is through a summer placement the previous year. Astra-Zeneca offers a summer placement during which the undergraduate can apply for a pre-registration placement and GlaxoSmithKline and Pfizer also offer summer internships and pre-registration placements. Six months of the pre-registration training must take place in a community or hospital setting.

There is a new centralised system for recruiting and selecting pre-registration pharmacists from 2017. Oriel, currently in existence for dentists, doctors and healthcare scientists, will be be used to recruit all hospital pre-registration trainees and the system is optional for community pharmacy.

In August 2017 Prospects stated that 'six months after graduating, 86.5% of pharmacy graduates are in full-time paid employment and 10.3% of graduates combine work and study, with 1.9% in further study. This means that over 96% of students go straight into employment. Of these, 98% take positions in the health sector.' While most students embark on a pharmacy degree with the direct intention of being employed as pharmacists, some may decide to go into research and development by taking an MSc or PhD. They may also decide to lecture students on pharmacy or related degree courses.

Most **community pharmacists** will work in independent pharmacies, which can range in size, some of them being family-run, with each generation qualifying in order to keep the business going. Others can be found attached to GP surgeries or health centres or are part of a large retail chain. Supermarkets increasingly have pharmacies in them to make it easier for patients to collect their medicines along with their shopping, particularly with the long opening hours. In smaller pharmacies, there may be only one or two pharmacists and one or two counter staff, whereas in a large business the pharmacist is also a manager in charge of many staff and needs to have business acumen. The job involves not only ensuring the safe dispensing of medicines, but providing advice to patients, health screening programmes, arranging for the delivery of prescriptions, monitoring of patients on long-term medication to ensure compliance and ringing GPs to clarify dosage and provide advice. In addition to being skilled in accuracy and using your knowledge of drugs and their effects, you also need to be confident in working with the general public, other professionals and the counter staff in order to enjoy a role as a community pharmacist.

As one of an estimated 6,000 pharmacists employed in hospitals, privately or in the NHS, you will be directly involved in the care of patients and a really important part of the healthcare team. You will attend ward rounds and work alongside the doctors to create treatments for patients. As medications and treatments become more complex, the **hospital pharmacist** has increasing levels of responsibility, for example, in adapting dosage to suit the needs of children and in supporting patients on long-term medications, helping them to manage side-effects. Aside from working on the wards, pharmacists will be involved with manufacturing sterile medicines, working in the dispensary, providing information on medicines and managing the purchase of medicines for the whole hospital. The opportunity to spend time on wards working with patients who have complex treatment needs is seen as one of the most rewarding aspects of the job, and doctors rely on pharmacists to ensure that prescriptions for patients in hospital and on discharge are accurately dispensed and that the patient can manage their medications.

Some pharmacists specialise as consultants in many areas such as haematology (blood), nephrology (kidneys), respiratory medicine, cardiology (heart), urology (urinary system), diabetes, gastroenterology (stomach and intestines), infectious diseases, paediatrics (children) and care of the elderly.

As a **primary care** pharmacist, you will be working alongside GPs in surgeries, supporting doctors in prescribing medicines and, as in the hospitals, supporting patients in managing their treatments. You are likely to build up longer-term relationships with patients than is often the case in a hospital setting. You are likely to be based within or close to the GP surgery.

There are increasingly opportunities as a qualified pharmacist to work with companies, for example, Interface Clinical Services, which are independent providers of clinical services in key areas of medicines management, long-term conditions and service redesign. Once you have experience of working as a pharmacist, especially in primary care or a hospital, a **clinical pharmacist** employed by such firms is able to be involved with services at all levels within the NHS, in addition to many joint initiatives with industry. Current projects in clinical pharmacy can be those dealing with osteoporosis, asthma, diabetes and stroke. You will work with a wide range of people in a range of roles, including practice managers, GPs, nurses, medicines management, CCGs (clinical commissioning groups), pharmaceutical representatives and hospitals. As the demands grow on the NHS for increasingly complex treatments, there will be more demand for highly qualified and experienced pharmacists to work in this field.

Unemployment rates among pharmacists are currently low, although there are concerns about the rising numbers of graduates in pharmacy, and the majority of graduates will get jobs in NHS hospitals or in the local high street chemist. Some will move into industry or stay in universities, doing further research or teaching students. A survey taken by the RPS states that as a qualified pharmacist you could probably expect a starting salary of around £20,000 to £30,000, depending on the area of pharmacy you choose to work in.

After 10 years you can expect to be earning anywhere between £35,000 and £60,000, whereas pharmacy technicians can expect a starting salary around £13,000 to £15,000, rising to £25,000 to £30,000 after 10 years. Prospects states that a pharmacist can expect to earn from £39,632 to £81,618 when fully qualified.

> 'Our MPharm graduates go into a number of different careers. Most will practise as a pharmacist in hospital or community pharmacy; however, a smaller number do go into the pharmaceutical industry. An increasing area of interest is primary care pharmacy or a GP Practice Pharmacist where they might train as independent prescribers managing the safe and effective use of medicines across the practice and ensuring prescribing is cost effective for the NHS. Pharmacists might run their own clinics, visit patients at home or in nursing or residential homes. Our graduates have also pursued careers in publishing, research, academia, management, and the armed forces.'
>
> Admissions Tutor, School of Pharmacy, University of Bradford

Continuing professional development

Following a revalidation consultation undertaken by the General Pharmaceutical Council in 2017, a new scheme will start in 2018 to ensure pharmacy professionals are continuing to meet the standards required for pharmacy professionals and that they are keeping their knowledge and skills up to date.

Up to 2017, pharmacists and pharmacy technicians were required to renew their registration annually, paying a fee and signing a declaration of their 'Fitness to practise'. They were expected to develop their skills and knowledge, making nine entries a year into a learning record; these could include researching a new drug, an aspect of management and running a business, or learning new skills as a result of a particular customer at the pharmacy. The pharmacist or pharmacy technician was not required to submit these every year, but they could be selected to produce their records at any time and their registration renewal could be in jeopardy if these did not meet the required standard.

In order to formalise this existing framework for continuing professional development (CPD) and maintain public confidence in the skills and knowledge of pharmacy professionals, from 2018 six records must be submitted each year and will include:

- four CPD records, with a minimum of two being planned learning activities
- one peer discussion
- one reflective account.

They will be submitted via a new online portal that is being launched with myGPhC in spring 2018.

Further details of the new scheme are available on the GPhC website and these will be updated as the new scheme is developed.

Q&A: GPhC

Will the new process for revalidating pharmacy professionals just apply to pharmacists?

No. The process will be the same for both pharmacists and pharmacy technicians. Collectively we call them pharmacy professionals. We consider both to be regulated professions and so they need to meet the same requirements in order to maintain their registration with us. However, the process has been designed so that it is flexible enough to work for both pharmacists and pharmacy technicians and also the wide range of roles that each profession performs.

Currently, to renew their registration, a pharmacist has to pay a fee and sign a fitness to practise form. Do they need to show evidence of CPD at present?

No. At the moment, there is no link between renewal of registration and our current CPD scheme. However, as part of revalidation and its introduction we are going to draw a link between renewal of registration and submission of the evidence to meet the requirements of revalidation. The processes for renewal and revalidation will continue to be separate but they will be timed to occur at the same time. That means that if someone has a legitimate reason for not being able to submit their revalidation information, they can ask for an extension or reduction in the requirements.

What CPD is available to pharmacists/pharmacy technicians and who provides it?

There is a wide range of ways that pharmacy professionals can undertake CPD and we do not stipulate a type of CPD activity we expect to be completed. Therefore, some CPD may not come from a provider but instead be work based or independent study for example. There are also a wide range of providers for CPD for pharmacy professionals. There might be education providers for post-registration training like an HEI or a government funded training provider like CPPE or NES as well as some private providers like CIG. There are also professional bodies (RPS and APTUK) operating in this space.

Case study: Pharmacy graduate in community pharmacy employment

Raveena Gill is the Pharmacy Manager in a community pharmacy in Tamworth, Staffordshire.

'I came to pharmacy through taking AS Physics and A level Biology, Chemistry, Mathematics and General Studies. After a work experience placement for a week at my uncle's pharmacy, I decided to apply for a pharmacy degree and was offered a place at the University of Portsmouth. Once I had qualified, I came back to the Midlands for my pre-registration training year in Tamworth and then worked as a locum in a number of pharmacies. I had an interview with Sainsbury's, but I decided I would prefer to work in an independent pharmacy as it gave me more opportunity to be involved with the business side of the practice. In Moxley, I was able to talk with staff in a care home to see what they needed with regard to medication and put procedures into place within the pharmacy. I particularly enjoyed the variety that this experience offered.

'I've now been qualified for eight years, and for the last five and a half years I've been the manager at a community pharmacy in Tamworth. It felt strange at first as this was the branch where I'd been a pre-registration trainee! I've learned a great deal about managing staff as well as dispensing medication and running health campaigns in this time. Through funding from the NHS Commissioning group, I've been trained to provide services such as emergency contraception and flu jabs (I've given 240 in the last four weeks!) and emergency medication for patients who have run out, usually over the weekend. We also run an asthma referral clinic and will often carry out blood pressure checks.

'My job as a pharmacist requires me to carry out CPD (continuing professional development) in order to maintain my registration with the General Pharmaceutical Council. At the moment, this involves making nine entries into my CPD log covering learning experiences such as developing my managerial role and learning about new drugs. We are a Healthy Living Pharmacy – a status that is now obligatory for all pharmacies in order to receive payments from the government – and we run different campaigns through the year. At the moment, we are running Mouth Cancer Awareness week and have posters in the pharmacy to encourage understanding of the possible symptoms. As the pharmacist, I am able to give advice to customers.

'At the moment, I enjoy my job and appreciate the stability it offers me, especially at a time of increasing competition for posts. The number of schools of pharmacy has increased over the last 10 years and there are so many well-qualified pharmacists completing their pre-registration training year that I would recommend pharmacy students do a variety of work placements through their degree, especially in the summer holidays, as these often lead to a pre-registration training placement.'

Further information

The internet is an excellent source of information and this section of the book lists useful contacts for you, whether you are interested in pharmacy or in pharmacology. The UCAS website is one of the most useful in terms of giving you information about courses (Course Search section) and their providers, as well as directing you to the universities' own websites. *HEAP 2018: University Degree Course Offers*, which is published by Trotman and written by Brian Heap, is a good source of information organised into subject areas, as is the *UCAS Guide to Getting into University and College*. Many students find the Student Room website (www.thestudentroom.co.uk) to be an accessible and user-friendly source of support, with forums to ask questions of students who either are in the process of making applications or have already done so. The information and advice given is, of course, only from individual experience and so may be subjective; it is always worthwhile contacting admissions tutors if you are in any doubt. It is in their interest to get the best possible students for their courses and to provide the information you need.

Important sources of information and support for pharmacy are as follows:

British Pharmaceutical Students' Association
The BPSA (www.bpsa.co.uk) aims to 'educate, represent and entertain its members throughout the MPharm degree until qualification'.

Formed in 1942, it solely represents pharmacy students and pre-registration pharmacists and has over 11,800 members. It has a Graduate Officer who supports students in getting pre-registration placements and in moving to employment. Its publication, *The Future Pharmacist* (archive editions on the BPSA website), gives useful advice to students applying and for undergraduates/pre-registration pharmacists.

General Pharmaceutical Council
The GPhC is the regulatory body for pharmacy, which provides accreditation for all pharmacy courses which qualify a graduate, following the pre-registration placement, to practise as a pharmacist. Accreditation reports, which are completed when a university establishes a new course, and regular reviews are available to read on the website by going to www.pharmacyregulation.org and clicking on the education section.

It was created, along with the Royal Pharmaceutical Society, in September 2010 when the previous Royal Pharmaceutical Society of Great

Britain was split so that representative and regulatory functions of the pharmacy profession could be separated. In addition to accrediting courses, it is also responsible for the independent regulation of the pharmacy profession within England, Scotland and Wales, being responsible for the regulation of pharmacists, pharmacy technicians and pharmacy premises. Its role is to protect the health, safety and well-being of people who use pharmacy services by registering competent professionals (pharmacists and pharmacy technicians) to practise pharmacy and by regulating the system for managing and delivering retail pharmacy services. Having these two regulatory roles makes the GPhC unique among the nine health professions regulators. Its address is:

The General Pharmaceutical Council
129 Lambeth Rd
London
SE1 7BT

Royal Pharmaceutical Society

A professional leadership body for pharmacists and pharmacy, its media centre has the latest pharmacy news and information about ongoing campaigns, for example 'Handwashing Essential Guide' in September 2017 and drugs safety updates and *Which* investigation into advice from pharmacies, with details of workshops to address issues and improve the advice patients get about medicines. Students can have membership at no cost if the university is accredited with the RPS. Its library is open for student enquiries: library@rpharm.com or 020 7572 2300. There is also an e-library that can be accessed by students and qualified pharmacy professionals.

Its website www.rpharms.com/careers is a useful source of information about different career options for pharmacists and of videos showing what pharmacists do. *Pharmacy Magazine* can be accessed through a free subscription service via www.pharmacymagazine.co.uk.

The **Pharmaceutical Society of Northern Ireland**, established in 1925, carries out the same regulatory functions as the GPhC. Its contact details are as follows:

Pharmaceutical Society of Northern Ireland
73 University Street
Belfast
BT7 1HL
info@psni.org.uk
028 9032 6927

National Pharmacy Association

This is a trade association for pharmacists which can be accessed via its website (www.npa.co.uk), but is more relevant to you when you are qualified and working in pharmacy.

Centre for Pharmacy Postgraduate Education (CPPE)

The CPPE offers continuing professional development and the BPSA has been working with it to allow students to access some of the materials it provides on specific topics. Topics covered have been as diverse as: Type 2 diabetes, Renal Medicine, NHS repeat dispensing, Patient Centred Care and, more recently, Healthy Living Pharmacies.

The United Kingdom Clinical Pharmacy Association (UKCPA)

This is a group aimed at pharmacists who want to develop and share clinical expertise and practice. It welcomes pharmacists from all areas of practice and organises conferences, publishes a newsletter and, critically, provides a forum for communication for clinical pharmacists from all over the country. It can be accessed through free electronic membership via the BPSA.

Industrial Pharmacy Brochure

This publication gives detailed advice, some applicable to pre-degree students, about placements and careers and can be accessed via the BPSA website.

Pharmacy Voice

The three largest community pharmacy associations have formed Pharmacy Voice to provide a forum for their members: Association of Independent Multiple Pharmacies (AIM), the Company Chemists' Association (CCA) and the National Pharmacy Association (NPA). Its publications can be found on its website (www.pharmacyvoice.com).

NHS

The NHS careers website is a useful source of information in terms of the roles undertaken by pharmacists, their training and the pre-registration year. Its website (www.healthcareers.nhs.uk/explore-roles/pharmacy) will give an insight into these areas.

Pre-registration placements from 2018 will be via a new online application process for pre-registration placements: Oriel (www.oriel.nhs.uk).

Prospects

Prospects describes itself as the official graduate careers website and it can be useful in seeing the opportunities open to qualified pharmacists. Details can be found via its website www.prospects.ac.uk.

Important sources of information and support for pharmacology are as follows:

British Pharmacological Society

Formed in 1931 the BPS, including its Clinical Pharmacology Section, is the professional association for pharmacologists in the UK and is one of the leading pharmacological societies in the world. It can be contacted via its website (www.bps.ac.uk) or at its London address:

The Schild Plot
16 Angel Gate
City Road
London
EC1V 2PT
Tel: 020 7239 0171

The Young Pharmacologists Advisory Group

This group is a core part of the British Pharmaceutical Society (BPS), includes around 600 undergraduates, postgraduates and recent graduates from 13 countries around the world and is active in the running of the Society. The Young Pharmacologists Advisory Group coordinates a number of projects to raise the profile of pharmacology by involving the society's younger members. These projects include networking events and bursaries for undergraduates. The BPS is also active in promoting careers for women in pharmacology.

Association of the British Pharmaceutical Industry

The Association of the British Pharmaceutical Industry (ABPI) states that it 'represents innovative research-based biopharmaceutical companies, large, medium and small, leading an exciting new era of biosciences in the UK. Our industry, a major contributor to the economy of the UK, brings life-saving and life-enhancing medicines to patients. Our members supply 90 per cent of all medicines used by the NHS, and are researching and developing over two-thirds of the current medicines pipeline, ensuring that the UK remains at the forefront of helping patients prevent and overcome diseases. The ABPI is recognised by government as the industry body negotiating on behalf of the branded pharmaceutical industry for statutory consultation requirements including the pricing scheme for medicines in the UK.' Its website (www.abpi.org.uk) provides information about its work and opportunities for employment.

For careers advice, go to www.careers.abpi.org.uk.

Glossary

ABPI (Association of the British Pharmaceutical Industry)

The trade association for 150 companies in the UK producing prescription medicines for humans.

ADHD (Attention Deficit Hyperactivity Disorder)

A group of behavioural symptoms that include inattentiveness, hyperactivity and impulsiveness.

Adjustment

The UCAS process by which a student who achieves higher than predicted grades can apply to other universities/courses. This process of trading up allows them to hold on to their existing place while they apply for a new one.

Aetiology

The science that deals with the causes or origin of disease.

BPS (British Pharmacological Society)

The professional association for pharmacologists in the UK, the Society aims to further education within pharmacology.

BPSA (British Pharmaceutical Students' Association)

The official student organisation of the Royal Pharmaceutical Society. The aim of the association is to 'educate, represent and entertain its members throughout the MPharm degree until qualification'.

Clearing

The UCAS process through which students not holding offers in August can apply for course vacancies.

CPPE (Centre for Pharmacy Postgraduate Education)

A not-for-profit organisation, funded by Health Education England, to offer continuing professional development opportunities for all pharmacists and pharmacy technicians providing NHS services in England.

Epidemiology

The study of the patterns, causes and effects of health and disease conditions in defined populations.

Extra

The UCAS facility available to students who are not holding offers by February of each application cycle that enables them to apply for the same course at other universities or different courses.

GPhC (General Pharmaceutical Council)

The body responsible for the independent regulation of the pharmacy profession (pharmacists, pharmacy technicians and pharmacy premises) within England, Scotland and Wales.

Neurodegenerative disease

An umbrella term for a range of conditions which primarily affect the neurons in the human brain.

NICE (National Institute for Health and Care Excellence)

A non-departmental public body of the Department of Health in the United Kingdom, it publishes guidelines on the use of health technologies within the NHS, clinical practice, guidance for public sector workers on health promotion and guidance for social care services and users.

Oriel

New online application system for pre-registration training placements.

OSPAP (Overseas pharmacists' assessment programme)

A postgraduate diploma that is undertaken as the first part of the route to registration required by those who have qualified as a pharmacist from outside of the European Economic Area. Five UK universities are accredited by the GPhC to offer this programme.

Personal statement

A statement written as part of the UCAS application which explains the reasons behind the applicant's desire to study the course, detailing relevant knowledge and skills.

Pharmacogenomics

The study of how a person's genes affect the way they respond to drugs.

Pharmacopoeia

A book containing directions for the identification of samples and the preparation of compound medicines.

POM

Prescription-only medicine.

Pre-registration year

The training year that takes place in a community or hospital pharmacy following completion of the MPharm degree, and which leads to registration with the General Pharmaceutical Council and full qualification as a pharmacist.

RPS or RPharmS (The Royal Pharmaceutical Society)

The body responsible for the leadership and support of the pharmacy profession within England, Scotland and Wales.

UCAS (Universities and Colleges Admissions Service)

The British admission service for students applying to university.

UKCPA (The United Kingdom Clinical Pharmacy Association)

A group aimed at pharmacists who want to develop and share clinical expertise and practice.

Walk-in centres

Provide a wide range of healthcare, advice and information for minor ailments, without the need for an appointment.